Diving Deep in Community Engagement

A Model for Professional Development

First Printing: 2015
ISBN 978-1-312-49960-7

Iowa Campus Compact
Pappajohn Education Center
1200 Grand Ave. Ste. 200
Des Moines, IA 50309
www.iacampuscompact.com

Editors: Mandi McReynolds and Emily Shields

Contributing Editors: J.R. Jamison and Amanda Wittman

Authors: Maggie Baker, Betsy Banks, Kate DeGraaf, Ashley Farmer-Hanson, Katie Halcrow, Laurel Hirt, and Nancy Mathias

Contributors: Maggie Grove, Julie Hatcher, Barbara Jacoby, Julia Mastronardi Yakovich, Agnieszka Nance, Julie Plaut, Heidi Pries, Andrew Seligsohn, Randy Stoecker, and Megan Voorhees

Graphic Designer: Lauren Oliver

Diving Deep in Community Engagement

A Model for Professional Development

Iowa | Campus Compact

Edited by Mandi McReynolds & Emily Shields

ACKNOWLEDGMENTS

ABOUT THE EDITORS

FOREWORD

REFLECTIONS FROM AN EDITOR

INTRODUCTION

TABLE OF ACTION

CHAPTER 1: INSTITUTIONAL STRATEGIC LEADER

CHAPTER 2: ORGANIZATIONAL MANAGER

CHAPTER 3: COMMUNITY INNOVATOR

CHAPTER 4: FIELD CONTRIBUTOR

CHAPTER 5: PROFESSIONAL DEVELOPMENT RESOURCES

Acknowledgments

Editors: Mandi McReynolds and Emily J. Shields

Contributing Editors: J.R. Jamison and Amanda Wittman

Copy Editor: Kristen Keener Pinheiro

Authors: Maggie Baker, Betsy Banks, Kate DeGraaf, Ashley Farmer-Hanson, Katie Halcrow, Laurel Hirt, and Nancy Mathias

Administrative Support: Justin Ellis

Contributors: Julie Hatcher, Barbara Jacoby, Julia Mastronardi Yakovich, Agnieszka Nance, Julie Plaut, Heidi Pries, Andrew Seligsohn, Randy Stoecker, and Megan Voorhees

Additional 2013 Diving Deep Institute Attendees: Christine Berg, Avery Brewton, Kathleen Brown, Mila Cooper, Cheri Doane, Brenna Hughes, Renee Sedlacek, Paul Simpson, Bridget Smith, Kristin Teig Torres, MaDonna Thelen, Gretchen Wehrle, Greg Welk, and Kate Willink

Graphic Designer: Lauren Oliver

Copyright Support: Dr. Marcia Keyser and her Spring 2014 "Copyright Issues" students, Drake University

This publication would not have been possible without the groundwork laid by the first and second Diving Deep Institutes, including support and leadership from Elaine Ikeda, Cathy Avila-Linn, Kathleen Rice, Julie Hatcher, J.R. Jamison, and Maggie Stevens.

About the Editors

Emily J. Shields is an experienced and recognized leader, manager, organizer, and advocate. She has served as executive director of Iowa Campus Compact (IACC) since 2011. Emily received a B.A. degree in journalism and political science from the University of Iowa and is pursuing a master's degree in philanthropy and nonprofit development at the University of Northern Iowa. Emily served as chief of staff for the Rebuild Iowa Office; a state agency created to coordinate Iowa's recovery from the 2008 disasters and was senate liaison and policy adviser to Iowa's governor. She has worked in field organizing and fundraising for political campaigns and served as an AmeriCorps VISTA member in San Antonio, Texas.

Emily serves on the Iowa Commission on Volunteer Service, the Governor's Council on the Expansion of National Service, and is involved with the Des Moines Young Nonprofit Professionals Network. She has been recognized as a *Des Moines Business Record* Forty Under 40 honoree, received the 2008 Governor's Excellence Award, and was a 2014 recipient of the AmeriCorps Alum Local Leadership Award. She enjoys reading, crossword puzzles, travel, and spending as much time as possible with her husband and two children.

Mandi McReynolds is an award-winning educator, author, and speaker. She has spent her career building service-learning and leadership programs at three institutions in Iowa. She received her B.A. from Cedarville University in organizational communication and her M.S. from Iowa State University with an emphasis in higher education, speech communication, and women's studies. In 2010-2011, she was named the Iowa Campus Compact Engaged Staff Award Winner. Mandi received the 2012 Iowa Student Personnel Association Outstanding Service Award. *The Des Moines Business Record* named Mandi to the 2015 list of Forty Under 40 honorees. Forty local business leaders, who were chosen by past award winners, are younger than 40 and have demonstrated impressive career achievements and unparalleled community involvement.

In 2014, she opened Mandi McReynolds Consulting focusing on supporting organizations in developing institutional strategies for community engagement and active-learning. In her free time, Mandi enjoys traveling with her husband Adam, swimming with her daughter Ava, and training for triathlons.

Foreword

Barbara Jacoby, Ph.D., Faculty Associate for Leadership and Community Service-Learning, Adele H. Stamp Student Union, University of Maryland

I never planned to be a community engagement professional. I had never heard the term "service-learning." All this changed rather dramatically for me one beautiful morning in May 1992. I was the director of the Office of Commuter Affairs at the University of Maryland, happily engaged with the myriad tasks of developing and implementing a wide range of programs and services for the majority of our students— including, of all things, the campus bus system. At 8:15 that morning, I arrived as usual in my office and began to unpack my briefcase before strolling to the coffee bar to get my morning fix. The phone on my desk rang. Only three people had that number: my mother, my husband, and my boss, the iconic Vice President for Student Affairs William L. "Bud" Thomas, Jr. It was Bud. Without any caffeine to bolster me, I heard him start speaking in his typical more-than-authoritative tone: "Barbara…" Yikes, I thought, he usually calls me Barb. What did I do? He continued, "I want you to take 'this volunteer/community service thing' into your office and make something of it." And he hung up the phone.

So began my career as a community engagement professional. Well, I thought, I've done some volunteer work. But I had no idea what I was to do in this new role of founding director of community service-learning at the University of Maryland. And there were few resources available to guide me as my colleagues and I sought to develop values, goals, and practices for our new area of responsibility.

We have come a long way. Service-learning is widely recognized as a high-impact educational practice, and there is no doubt in my mind that it is now permanently part of the landscape of higher education. We have amassed considerable evidence of its benefits for students and communities. Service-learning is embedded in the curriculum and the co-curriculum, organizational infrastructure, base budgets, long-term campus-community partnerships, faculty research, and even the tenure and promotion process. Our institutions engage with our communities in deep and meaningful ways to achieve shared goals and to promote sustainable economic development. Happily, for those of us who find ourselves—either by choice or fiat—in the role of community engagement professional, many excellent resources exist in the form of books, journals, conferences, workshops, listservs, peer support programs, and more. Campus Compact has expanded from 113 member institutions to nearly 1,100 member institutions and 34 offices of its state network. It provides and supports a wide range of professional development and other resources and opportunities for those of us who are just dipping our toes into the water, as well as "old-timers" like me who are seeking to enhance and enrich our work. Campus Compact offers a workshop for new community service-learning professionals, Diving In: Institute for New Community Service-Learning Professionals, together with an accompanying guide, *Looking In Reaching Out.* Its Diving Deep Institute for Experienced Civic and Community Engagement Practitioners gave rise to this newest resource.

I welcome and appreciate this publication for the wise advice and specific examples it offers to guide us in being successful in the multiple, complex, and challenging roles that we play as community engagement professionals, whether our work focuses on service-learning or more broadly on community engagement. I have learned much from the outstanding leaders in our field who have generously shared their experiences with us. I particularly value the emphasis on an additional role that we all must assume if we are going to realize the tremendous potential of community engagement for all its stakeholders: that of reflective practitioner. As busy as we are, as full of sometimes-conflicting demands as our days can be, we must walk the walk of critically reflecting on our work, as we encourage our students to do. Many of us who have engaged our students in service-learning reflection are familiar with the classic prompt: What have we done and learned? So what does it mean? Now what do we do about it? I believe these questions also serve us well as we reflect on our work, both on our campuses and nationally through organizations such as Campus Compact. The reflection questions this book provides in relation to each of the professional roles it describes are exactly what we need to deeply and critically reflect on the complexities and dilemmas of our work.

In the preface to my recent book, *Service-Learning Essentials: Questions, Answers, and Lessons Learned,* I make the point that service-learning and community engagement in higher education will survive and thrive into the future because we continue to ask questions—fundamental and straightforward, demanding and challenging—about its purpose and value, how to do it and how to do it better, how we will know whether it makes any difference, and how the powerful combination of service and learning can catalyze broader and deeper engagement between higher education institutions and communities in our own backyards and around the world. It is reflection and questioning that will enable us to move our work forward, to shape its direction and focus. Without addressing the big questions, we risk the potential of "just doing" or, worse yet, doing harm by exploiting the goodwill of our community partners and perpetuating the wrongful view that service is the most effective means of addressing our most pressing social issues.

Henry A. Giroux (2002), a provocateur about higher education's role in society, reminds us that higher education is "one of the few public spaces left where students can learn the power of questioning authority, recover the ideals of engaged citizenship, reaffirm the importance of the public good, and expand their capacities to make a difference" (p. 450). Our role as community engagement professionals in influencing higher education to fulfill this public purpose cannot be underestimated. But, like you, I know all too well that the work of creating courses, programs, and environments that provide transformative learning experiences for our students, while also working to transform our communities for the better, is very hard work. We want to move our work forward, but sometimes we feel like Sisyphus pushing that rock up the hill. Also, let's face it, work in the trenches of community engagement is often messy. It involves big ideals and goals, but our daily tasks can be difficult, frustrating, time consuming, and just plain gritty (e.g., "I thought you brought the work gloves."). However, we feel we are well-supported and in good company, thanks to our colleagues who shared their thoughtful reflections, case studies, and questions with us in this volume. To them and to you, I offer the inspiring words of the late singer-songwriter Pete Seeger: "Any one of us might be the grain of sand to make the scales go the right way" (Whitehead, 2006).

Reference

Giroux, H. A. (2002). Neoliberalism, corporate culture, and the promise of higher education, *Harvard Educational Review, 4*(72), 425-463.

Whitehead, J. (2006). When will they ever learn? An interview with Pete Seeger. The Rutherford Institute. Retrieved from http://www.therutherford.org.

Reflections From an Editor

Mandi McReynolds

At the beginning of a new endeavor with students, faculty, or community partners, I share the following story titled *One Sweet Deal!*

In the early 1600s, Great Britain and Holland spent years competing for treasured spices found on a few tiny islands in the East Indies. The island named Run became a point of contention when British Captain Nathaniel Courthope staked a claim on it. The island contained one of the only known nutmeg forests. In 1620 the Dutch, through the use of a spy, seized and murdered the captain. They were able to take over the island with all of its luxurious spices. The island became a source of bitterness for the British. When the two countries prepared the peace treaty, the Dutch offered a remote island named Manhattan. A place only inhabited by just a handful of individuals and located near a place called Staten Island (Beyer, 2003).

What did it take to make Manhattan the thriving metropolis it is today? It took dreamers, explorers, and individuals willing to envision a future for a vast and desolate island. I ponder frequently: What is the "Manhattan" for community engagement in higher education? We are a field with a relatively young history. Many new areas of leadership are still to be explored, developed, and built by practitioner-scholars in community engagement. Our history is built on individuals who chose to create and not be defined by standard cultural norms (you will find many of them as authors, editors, and contributors within this book). As we embark on being catalysts for cultivating transformational institutional and community change, should we dare lay the trail for these leadership roles within the academy or units not yet defined? I say, "Absolutely! Unequivocally, yes!"

One "Manhattan" is for leadership in higher education to consider the role of a community engagement professional and/or unit for community engagement. As the field of service-learning and community-based learning is expanding, the opportunity for growth and leadership is beginning to form. Butin (2010) discusses the service-learning movement as following in the footsteps and patterns of the women's studies movement in higher education. First, the movement started with a few scholars, conferences, workshops, and external funding support. Then, it gained momentum through interdisciplinary scholars recognizing their support and role of the work and the explosion of theoretical scholarship. Just as the feminist movement transitioned from intellectual movement to academic discipline, so could service-learning and community-based learning in the next 15 years.

The future could hold more majors and minors in community engagement or deans of community-based education. A few innovative universities such as University of Wisconsin-Milwaukee and Northern Kentucky University have begun to create executive-level positions such as "chief public engagement officer" in the roles of chancellors, vice presidents, or associate provosts. The people in these roles oversee the collaborations of community-based learning, co-curricular service, and community relations. They also support a holistic view of institutions becoming engaged in their communities and returning to the role of contributing to the common good (Beere, Votruba, & Wells, 2011). As a field, we must be prepared for these new roles of leadership and units within the academy. According to Campus Compact's 2012 annual survey, most of these positions are still mid-level directorships or entry-level coordinator positions. As these positions and divisions have emerged over the years, a limited amount of resources have been developed to support the personal and professional growth of these roles and units. For the success of community engagement and cultivating engaged campuses across the country, it is crucial for those in the field to set a guiding framework for professionals and units.

When I applied to attend the Campus Compact Diving Deep Institute in 2013, I saw this vast land. It was my desire to support the field in cultivating a practitioner-scholar-focused publication on the role of community engagement professionals. I entered the institute and worked with the facilitators on crafting an outline for collecting data from the other seasoned practitioners in the field who were attending the institute. At the end of the session and the data collection, we asked those who were interested to stay and discuss developing a resource for the field. To my surprise, 14 practitioner-scholars stayed to envision the work of *Diving Deep in Community Engagement: A Model for Professional Development*. They were committed to serving as architects for this "Manhattan."

As I sit typing this final reflection and get this publication ready for the final stages of editing, I am filled with deep emotion and admiration for our team. We have all worked together for more than a year to produce the publication. It has pushed each of us to reflect on our own work, institutional community engagement, and the direction of the field. Our common purpose is to see institutions and communities transformed through community engagement. The essence of community engagement calls for the institution to act on its civic purpose and social compact responsibilities to the common good. The framework outlined in these chapters is mission-critical for cultivating higher education civic values.

Now tugging at my leg is my inquisitive five-year-old daughter asking me, "What are you doing?" It prompts me to think. What will she say in 13 years? How will she describe her mother and her work? It is my hope she will say, "My mother is an innovative leader in higher education and community engagement. She was an explorer who saw a vast island needing to be revitalized. She built with her colleagues across the country a framework for professionals in a thriving metropolis called "Community Engagement in Higher Education." Together, they started the movement in Iowa at an institute. The reason our college or university has a professional and unit focused on community engagement is because *they decided it was time to dive deep and grow the profession!*"

References

Beyer, R. (2003). *The greatest stories never told: Tales from history to astonish, bewilder, and stupefy.* New York, NY: Harper Collins.

Beere, C.A., Votruba, J.C., & Wells, G.W. (2011). Becoming an engaged campus: A practical guide for institutionalizing public engagement. San Fransico, CA: Jossey-Bass.

Butin, D. W. (2010). *Service-learning in theory and practice.* New York, NY: Palgrave MacMillan.

Campus Compact. (2012). *2012 annual membership survey.* Boston, MA.

Introduction

Purpose

Collectively, the practitioner-scholars who designed and created this book have more than 240 years of experience in the field of higher education community engagement. The purpose of this publication is to support those working in, leading, and otherwise advancing this field. We have included various voices from the field, and each chapter contains its own unique reflections from seasoned practitioners.

Our goals in this publication are to:

- Suggest a comprehensive framework for the knowledge, skills, and "competencies" professionals in the field of community engagement need, regardless of specialization or positional role

- Help guide support and professional development for practitioners, leaders, and professionals

- Move the field forward and encourage practitioner-scholarship

- Serve as an example of collaborative practitioner-scholarship

We want to make a note about some of the main terms we chose. One thing we can say with certainty about this field is that it has not come to consensus on language. We respect and appreciate this diversity and hope you will see it reflected throughout this publication. To help encompass all those who may consider themselves to be included in this field, we use the term *community engagement professional.* Our intention is to recognize that this work has moved beyond what is traditionally referred to as "service-learning" and includes a variety of roles related to community and civic engagement, service, and volunteerism. We use the term interchangeably recognizing the practice may differ among institutions, communities, roles, and contexts.

We frequently use the term "practitioner-scholarship" and "practitioner-scholar" to describe this role and our goals. Charles McClintock (2004) defines the scholar-practitioner as "an ideal of professional excellence grounded in theory and research, informed by experimental knowledge, and motivated by personal values, political commitments, and ethical conduct" (p. 393). This professional model is used in teacher education (Wunder & Macintyre Latta, 2012), clinical psychology (Stoltenburg, Pace, Kashubeck-West, Biever, Patterson, & Welch, 2000), nursing (Peterson & Jones, 2013), and management (Salipante & Aram, 2003). A practitioner-scholar has the unique ability to perceive deficiencies in current theories and practices through his or her own direct experience. Their research and pedagogical knowledge is fundamentally needed to challenge and drive the development of a stronger academy (Bringle & Hatcher, 2009; Ospina & Dodge, 2005). Similar to the typology of service-learning (Sigman, 2004), practitioner-scholar uses a hyphen to create one word describing the equal and mutually beneficial role of both professional responsibilities in one person.

The Process

In July 2013, Diving Deep: Campus Compact's Third Institute for Experienced Civic and Community Engagement Practitioners was held in Des Moines, Iowa. This week-long event built on the traditions of previous institutes held in California in 2010 and Indiana in 2011. The institute was envisioned in the original curriculum as a place where a community of change agents from the field of service-learning and civic and community engagement can deepen our capacity as transformational leaders to advance the work on our campuses and with our communities. The 2013 Institute brought together 23 practitioners with at least five years of experience and four facilitators. They represented a broad range of institutions and administrative roles within the field of community engagement, service-learning, and civic education. As a brainstorming activity, the group was asked to discuss and document the common competencies and areas of professional growth for the future of the field.

Afterward, a smaller group of those who elected to participate further analyzed the overall themes collected from the institute and reviewed the current literature and research related to professional competencies, job descriptions, standards and roles of community engagement professionals or similar fields, such as nonprofit volunteer managers, chief community engagement officers, and student affairs professionals. In September 2013, the collaborative of editors and authors gathered to review the framework of spheres for this model and made the decision to develop a publication for current professionals, those who support their work, and aspiring professionals to support their growth and advancement and the larger field of community engagement in higher education. It is important to note that students were key collaborators in the project. A Drake University course served as a copyright review board, and a Drake University student served as senior graphic designer for the project.

From the research and participant practice analysis, four key "spheres" were constructed to represent the role of the community engagement professional: institutional strategic leader, organizational manager, community innovator, and field contributor. These spheres are interconnected and work collectively to cultivate the role of a community engagement professional.

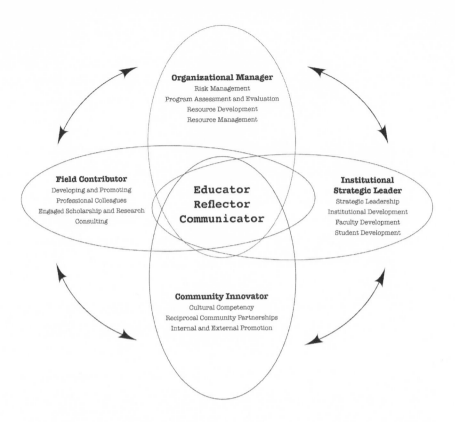

Institutional Strategic Leader is defined as someone who provides the vision, knowledge, skills, and relationships to align resources and help the institution achieve its goals for community engagement, living up to its ideals.

Organizational Manager is defined as someone who is highly skilled in assessment; resource development; and organizational management, which includes human resources, risk management, and program management.

Community Innovator is defined as someone who is skilled in leveraging the human and social capital of an institution of higher education. This is accomplished by building partnerships aimed at pursuing innovative solutions to challenges faced by individuals in a community, dually focused on educating students and impacting communities.

Field Contributor is defined as someone who is able to provide encouragement, mentorship, research, data, consulting, or other aspects that contribute to increasing positive change in the field of civic engagement.

Each sphere contains carefully crafted subcategories for professional development focus to support overall skill and knowledge growth.

In our discussions and analysis, we also determined there are three other areas in which a community engagement professional will need skills and knowledge. These areas over-arch and cross through all of the other spheres of the framework and are the roles of a reflector, educator, and communicator.

Reflection is a key component in the field of community engagement. It is the thread that ties knowledge to the work at hand and challenges our educational growth. As practitioners in the field, we have responsibility to strive to reflect and inspire reflection in others. No matter which sphere we are working within, structured and intentional reflection is imperative to the advancement of one's practice.

Education is the cornerstone of supporting the knowledge and practice of skill development. We are responsible to be lifelong learners in our field. As you read the resources and reflection questions within the chapters, you will find the authors and editors intentionally used the term "advanced" and provided suggestions even for those far along in their careers. We are never finished learning. You will find suggested "beyond the typical" growth experiences that will provide professionals, supervisors, and units opportunities outside traditional professional development tracks. These experiences can bring fresh perspective and support for continuing the educational process in each frame.

The *Diving Deep* practitioner-scholars shared in the analysis process of the framework how the role of a community engagement professional can be ambiguous. As a young field, many practitioners were the first person in their role at their institution or have a supervisor who had limited knowledge of the field. It is imperative to recognize the educational process is not just about retaining knowledge or a skill within each sphere. It involves educating others through sharing, mentoring, and cultivating best practices.

Communication is foundational to serving as a boundary-spanning unit or professional. For an institutional strategic leader, communication is designed to support casting and advocating for the vision of community engagement within the institution. For an organizational manager, communication is needed as a primary function to run the day-to-day operations. For a community innovator, communication transcends barriers between the institution and the community. For a field contributor, communication is needed to mentor others and contribute to the body of knowledge within community engagement. Communication is an essential component throughout each sphere.

Intended Audience & Use

This publication is designed to be pliable and reflective. Ultimately, it should support others in "diving deep." We hope it will serve presidents, unit or division leaders, supervisors, and current and future practitioners by providing a framework for the role and professional growth of a community engagement professional. We provide a table of action and professional development resources list to serve as a launching point for charting a continued path for development.

In the spring of 2014, the editors and authors hosted a webinar and several professional development sessions based on the framework. Practitioners and administrators responded with how they envision the publication being used as a resource, including to:

- Draft position descriptions
- Provide a framework for a community engagement office/ division/unit staffing structure
- Provide a framework for an annual report on community engagement

- Demonstrate the need for resources in the area of service-learning, community engagement, and civic engagement

- Examine campus and community barriers that could hinder community engagement professionals from serving as effective advocates and leaders in civic engagement

- Support community engagement professionals in employee evaluation and expectation review

- Provide justification for professional development expenses for community engagement professionals

- Support construction of professional development plans for individuals and units

- Provide a framework for mentorship in the field

- Provide a framework for scholarship and research to be conducted in the field of community engagement professionals

- Support the alignment of web-based materials, conferences, publications, and resources related to the competency areas

- Assist in educating institutions and the community about the vital and complex role of community engagement professionals

- Guide community engagement professionals in developing a résumé or portfolio of professional accomplishments and skill sets

- Support the development of undergraduate or graduate educational opportunities that discuss community engagement as a vocation

Our goal is not to insert into the field one framework that applies to all roles and institutions related to community engagement. We desire to push the level of reflection and conversation to advance the field. The chapters are designed to evoke a critical reflective response from readers. Each chapter contains reflection questions, case studies, and a field leader's critical response. These are to be used to support a deeper reflective analysis of the sphere and challenge one to think about examples and alternative views related to each frame.

Our goal is for *Diving Deep in Community Engagement: A Model for Professional Development* to grow and change with the field as it embarks on the 21st century. Our goal is also to support further practitioner-scholarship in this field and serve as an example of the type of collaborative approach that can be successful. Those staffing and coordinating this work on a daily basis possess knowledge, data, and other information. It needs to be shared, and we seek ways to support them in collecting and disseminating that work. We hope this framework will serve as a platform for elevating professionals, this field, and our collective voice and vision.

References

Bringle, R.G., & Hatcher, J.A. (2009). Innovative practices in service-learning and curricular engagement. *New Directions for Higher Education, 2009*(147), 37-46.

McClintock, C. (2004). The scholar-practitioner model. In A. DiStefano, K.E. Rudestam, & R.J. Silverman (Eds.), *Encyclopedia of distributed learning* (393-396). Thousand Oaks, CA: Sage Publications.

Ospina, S. M., & Dodge, J. (2005). Narrative inquiry and the search for connectedness: Practioners and academics developing public administration scholarship. *Narrative Inquiry and the Search for Connectedness, 65*(4), 409-423.

Peterson, K., & Jones, S. (2013). Integrating the scholarship of practice into the nursing academician portfolio. *Journal of Nursing Education and Practice 3*(11), 84-92.

Salipante, P., & Aram, J.D. (2003). The nature of practitioner-scholar research in the nonprofit sector. *NonProfit Management & Leadership, 14*(2), 139-150.

Sigmon, R. (1994). Serving to learn, learning to serve in promoting school success. *Linking Service with Learning.* Council of Independent Colleges monograph.

Stoltenberg, C.D., Pace, T.M., Kashubeck-West, S., Biever, J.L., Patterson, T., & Welch, I.D. (2000). Training models in counseling psychology: Scientist-practitioner versus practitioner-scholar. *The Counseling Psychologist, 28*(5), 622-640.

Wunder, S.A., & Macintyre Latta, M. (2012). *Placing practitioner knowledge at the center of teacher education: Rethinking the policies and practices of the education doctorate.* Charlotte, NC: Information Age Publishing, Inc.

Table of Action

Vision without action is a daydream.
Action without vision is a nightmare.
Japanese Proverb

[Editor's note: This introduction was primarily authored by Mandi McReynolds. The table of action includes contributions from all editors and authors.]

I love to swim. I grew up around the water and learned to swim at a very young age. The water has always been a place of freedom, calmness, and reflection. Diving into the water is an exhilarating feeling. It creates a surge of energy. I will never forget the memory of my first dive. At the age of two, I stood at the edge of a diving board and looked deep into the water. The three-meter springboard distance seemed like a mile. The water seemed as though it was ocean depth.

It was my first dive into the pool. The rush of excitement went all over my body. A shiver so deep ran down my barely two-and-a-half-foot spine. The chill reached to the innermost part of my back. I am sure the ruffle on my red polka-dotted swimsuit was shaking. My mom was on the sidelines holding her breath. My sister was waiting at the side of the pool to see if I could do it. I had watched them time and again jump into the pool. I knew it was possible. I knew the water would not swallow me whole. It was all up to me. It was my time to be brave and act. I closed my eyes, clasped my hands above my head in a shark-like position, and leaped. *SPLASH!* One act of bravery gave me the courage to continue diving and swimming for 30 more years.

Today, I am still developing my technique as a swimmer. I have had many belly flops and imperfect moments swimming, but the water remains a place of refuge and personal growth. Careers often take similar paths. We can read, research, attend conferences, and reflect, but eventually we must act. It is imperative for our growth to begin and continue. Concrete action pushes us toward meeting the critical vision and mission of higher education's civic purpose. Some of us may be clasping our hands above our heads and striving to take that first leap by developing programs. Others may have 30 years in the field and are refining their technique by pushing campuses to think about their role as anchor institutions in the community. Each of us must begin to map our training plan. Being a practitioner-scholar means we practice the profession through a critical lens.

Are you ready to leap? While critical reflection is important (and, indeed, a focus of this publication), concrete action steps are critical. To this end, we collaborated to concisely suggest key actions and activities that a practitioner could undertake to develop professional competence in each sphere. These actions provide specific ideas of activities designed to support growth in the field. We envision community engagement professionals using these actions to help build a professional development plan. Similarly, administrators can use them as signposts to think about the development of staff and offices.

Each sphere is laid out on a spectrum, representing the development of a community engagement professional from novice to advanced. Taking on more advanced activities usually requires a solid foundation and knowledge in each sphere, and many of the activities for advanced professionals revolve around sharing experiences and knowledge at the field level and beyond. Community engagement professionals using this as a guide should not be surprised if they are advanced in one area and novice in another. All professionals come to this work from varied backgrounds that provide diverse skills and training. However, advancing in all the spheres will help professionals become well-rounded and comfortable in supporting the university in meeting its civic mission and purpose.

This table of action represents the collective wisdom of the editors, authors, and contributors of this volume. These are not meant to be read as the only actions a professional should take to develop along his or her career path, but they should be seen as a starting point for reflection upon building a career as a community engagement professional. Take what works for you and add your own ideas as you consider how the model we are presenting could benefit your career and impact this field. Like any excellent diver, enjoy the process, ask questions, focus on flexibility, fine-tune your technique, and above all else

...leap.

Institutional Leader Table of Action
Strategic Leadership

Novice

Develop a personalized leadership development plan to capitalize on strengths and identify partners to complement areas of weakness.

Understand the culture and politics of your institution and develop key relationships and partnerships to build or expand an engagement program.

Demonstrate skills in strategic thinking and planning, assessment, and reporting.

Intermediate

Create a support system to implement and sustain your personal and professional development by working with a team or coach.

Understand strategic leadership as it works in higher education, as well as other types of organizations.

Balance between big-picture vision of the institution and daily operations.

Advanced

Train and coach others to apply strategic leadership skills through community engagement.

Develop, manage, assess, report, and recognize contributors to change processes, while effectively balancing goals and relationships to maintain progress toward priorities.

Intentionally engage with other senior-level administrators to ensure community engagement priorities are met.

Institutional Leader Table of Action

Institutional Development

Novice

Learn about the history of engagement at the institution.

Map out current curricular and co-curricular service initiatives and compare them to national benchmarks and standards.

Identify and consult with stakeholders to inform decisions.

Collaborate with other campus service and community-based programs.

Learn about the institution's priorities and discuss with key leaders how engagement can support those.

Intermediate

Provide training and development for student program leaders.

Develop institutional assessment to measure service impact across programs.

Centralize and coordinate key functions for engagement.

Implement discipline- or division-wide strategies that provide pathways for engagement.

Engage stakeholders by developing a formal advisory committee.

Create program visibility by inviting key administrators to speak at events and participate in site visits.

Advanced

Identify and develop institutional strategic partnerships in the community.

Advance community engagement and/or community-based learning through resources, visibility, donor engagement, etc.

Coordinate strategic planning efforts to move vision and goals forward.

Provide leadership to develop the institution's mission, vision, and strategic plan, as they relate to community engagement and civic education.

Institutional Leader Table of Action

Faculty Development

Novice

Understand curriculum development, learning objectives, and assessment.

Build partnerships and create allies with chief academic officer and key faculty.

Assess faculty interest in service-learning and communicate how it can meet their instructional goals.

Support faculty already engaged in service-learning.

Provide logistical assistance for service-learning courses.

Understand the institution's culture and norms, policies, and practices that impact faculty receptiveness to community engagement work.

Intermediate

Support and develop faculty skills in designing service-learning course/s and locating community partners.

Train faculty to incorporate service-learning in their course/s, scholarship, research, and disciplines by providing workshops or a campus-wide seminar series.

Design effective community-based learning experiences by collaborating with faculty.

Build collegial relationships with faculty by attending meetings and/or serving on academic committees.

Advanced

Teach or co-teach a service-learning course.

Partner with faculty leaders to enact structures and incentives that institutionalize service-learning, such as tenure and promotion, engaged scholarship, and community-based research.

Collaborate with departments and to embed service-learning and engaged scholarship practices that strategically work toward a greater collective impact of the institution in the community and with students.

Institutional Leader Table of Action

Student Development

Novice

Understand various theories and models related to student development, learning, and experiential learning.

Design and facilitate service programs, orientation, reflection, and evaluation to attain both specific learning outcomes and provide needed service to the community.

Train student service leaders in the basics of organizing and leading quality service programs.

Supervise, advise, and develop student leaders in civic engagement programs.

Intermediate

Coach and mentor students to develop advanced leadership skills in both academic and co-curricular service programs.

Collaborate with curricular and co-curricular programs to promote student leadership in engagement programs.

Use student leaders on advisory boards, as service-learning assistants, and as community liaisons.

Advanced

Mentor students interested in the civic engagement field.

Create opportunities for students to have a voice and leadership in institutional direction for community engagement.

Engage students in national and international networks for community engagement and support implementation of their ideas on campus.

Evaluate and assess student programs to improve learning outcomes and student development objectives and report results.

Organizational Manager Table of Action

Risk Management

Novice

Understand risk management needs for specific programs and events.

Develop background knowledge of applicable policies or laws.

Intermediate

Understand overall institutional approach to risk management and applicable policies, rules, and laws.

Be familiar with community partner needs and policies.

Review institutional liability and insurance information to ensure university and community coverage is adequate for community engagement.

Advanced

Develop a comprehensive risk management framework of policies, procedures, waivers, contracts, and agreements to protect the institution, faculty, administration, students, and community.

Respond to different needs as they arise and understand policies and laws.

Develop a comprehensive risk management and liability committee to review and assess ongoing efforts.

Conduct trainings for campus and community stakeholders on risk assessment policies, actions, and plans.

Organizational Manager Table of Action

Program Assessment and Evaluation

Novice

Investigate assessment and evaluation and the difference between the two.

Obtain knowledge of institutional assessment and evaluation efforts.

Conduct post-program, -course, and -event evaluations.

Intermediate

Successfully evaluate comprehensive programming.

Incorporate institutional community engagement assessment and evaluation into existing institutional research and assessment efforts.

Conduct both formative and summative evaluation.

Advanced

Focus on comprehensive institution-wide assessment and evaluation of community engagement, including students, faculty, staff, and community voice.

Develop impact and assess measurement practices for evaluating holistic engagement efforts.

Contribute to campus-wide evaluation and assessment efforts and effectively communicate results of engagement activities.

Use data to apply for national recognition.

Organizational Manager Table of Action

Resource Development

Novice

Develop knowledge of one or two fundraising methods, such as grant writing for small programs, events, or course-based experiences.

Work with students, faculty, and staff to fund-raise for small-scale community engagement efforts.

Intermediate

Conduct development planning with multiple partners and develop sustainable funding sources for programming, events, and activities.

Use multiple fundraising methods to diversify funding.

Research major gift opportunities and review prospective funding sources.

Advanced

Successfully secure and maintain sustainable funding sources to support strategic partnerships and advance the civic purpose of the institution.

Leverage strong relationships with on-campus development staff and administrative leadership to articulate engagement's connection to institutional fundraising priorities.

Seek funding through innovative channels, such as statewide or national initiatives, endowment funding, or social venture programs.

Organizational Manager Table of Action

Resource Management

Novice

Investigate human and other resource management frameworks and strategies.

Supervise the work of others.

Serve as a leader on a taskforce, committee, or council on campus.

Intermediate

Understand your role in resource management within the larger institutional context.

Implement strong management practices that align with institutional policies and priorities.

Use techniques in motivation and performance measurement.

Advanced

Lead and manage large teams of faculty, staff, administrators, and strategic community partners on mutually beneficial institutional and community initiatives.

Strategically use resources to achieve long-term goals and outcomes of community engagement.

Intentionally leverage resources to impact social change on campus and in the community through community and economic development.

Community Innovator Table of Action

Cultural Competency

Novice

Know and use the history, culture, and identity of the college/university to understand how they each intersect with the community and sub-communities within it.

Identify key stakeholders, both internal and external to the institution, that will promote cultural awareness and sensitivity, while being cognizant of reciprocity with partners in the community.

Intermediate

Seek out opportunities to be immersed in the community to develop an understanding of various cultures existing within the larger community and among community partner organizations.

Inquire and seek to understand how changes in programming, courses, curricula and, external activities at the college/university may lead to more culturally sensitive approaches to community outreach.

Involve internal and external stakeholders in a process of reviewing institutional and community culture.

Advanced

Encourage critical evaluation of procedures, habits, and policies that may be culturally insensitive to the community of which the institution is a member.

Collaborate with faculty, staff, and administrators to design/redesign courses, curricula, programs, and external campaigns that are sensitive to the institution's role as a reciprocal partner and member of the community.

Create spaces for campus and community members to collaboratively investigate cultural differences.

Community Innovator Table of Action

Reciprocal Community Partnerships

Novice

Identify existing needs and assets in the community and at the college/university in preparation to develop and foster reciprocal relationships in campus-community partnerships.

Design a way to evaluate the degree of reciprocity among existing community partnerships.

Intermediate

Conduct ongoing evaluation of reciprocity in campus-community partnerships.

Recognize and foster partnerships focused on shared measurement goals of community impact.

Advanced

Collaborate with community partners and senior administrators to engage in collective impact around relevant and pressing social issues in your community.

Collaborate with partners to create a system of shared measurement of community impact.

Community Innovator Table of Action
Internal and External Promotion

Novice

Articulate to internal/external stakeholders the impact various activities/courses/curricula/programs have on the community beyond your campus.

Assist internal and external audiences in their understanding of the wider implications of civic engagement beyond the borders of your campus.

Establish engagement activities and partnerships to introduce community partners to the institution.

Intermediate

Facilitate college faculty and staff understanding of the institution as a partner in the community; provide language, information, and assistance for them to tell this story to outside stakeholders, leading to new partnerships.

Create and participate in opportunities that allow your institution to play a role in collective impact around social issues, increasing the reach of your institution.

Encourage the institution to leverage assets (i.e., knowledge, talent, facilities, etc.) contributing toward collective impact in the community.

Advanced

Strategically promote campus personnel's connection to engagement; inform external stakeholders and seek their collaboration in these activities.

Gather stakeholders in the community to engage in collective impact around social issues; share stories of collaboration and impact with larger communities.

Tell positive stories of programmatic and curricular changes at your institution that are tethered to working toward collective impact in your community and how they enhance student learning.

Field Contributor Table of Action

Developing and Promoting Professional Colleagues

Novice

Mentor students.

Conduct trainings for students in service-learning graduate programs.

Nominate individuals for recognition.

Write recommendations for students.

Coach individuals on résumé, cover letter, interviewing, and overall job search.

Intermediate

Coach a new community engagement professional at another institution.

Serve as a mentor at the International Association for Research on Service-Learning and Community Engagement or other related conference.

Nominate individuals for state-wide or national awards.

Introduce students to colleagues and networks in the field.

Advanced

Mentor undergraduates and graduate students wanting to enter the field.

Teach graduate courses on service learning.

Serve on an awards selection committee at the state or national level.

Field Contributor Table of Action

Engaged Scholarship and Research

Novice

Learn the language and differences between various types of scholarship.

Read journals and attend annual national conferences to become better acquainted with what people are doing research on and where the gaps exist.

Learn the language of program evaluation and assessment to better understand the needs of the field and the role you can play.

Write and submit a conference proposal.

Participate in a research project.

Create intentional professional development time for cultivating practitioner-scholarship.

Intermediate

Assist in developing institutional assessment of programs.

Be a proposal reviewer or serve on a conference planning team.

Take a research methods course.

Be a contributor to your state Campus Compact website or blog.

Evaluate new methods of inquiry and dissemination for practitioner-scholarship.

Advanced

Form new partnerships with your institutional research office.

Consider participating in collective research.

Author or co-author an article for publication.

Initiate and edit a collection of practitioner-scholarship engagement stories from the field.

Cultivate new ways of knowing through innovative practitioner-scholarship research and dissemination practices.

Field Contributor Table of Action

Consulting

Novice

Connect to a formalized group to share with local colleagues/institutions about programs.

Share your efforts to develop programming.

Participate in a grant review process.

Intermediate

Work with another institution to develop its own civic engagement department.

Develop and share a model of good practice with other campuses.

Participate in a state-wide grant review process.

Represent your colleagues in the state on a committee or board where you actively seek their feedback and make decisions for the collective.

Advanced

Become part of an external review committee for another institution.

Develop a capacity-building program, institute, or workshop.

Participate in a national grant review process.

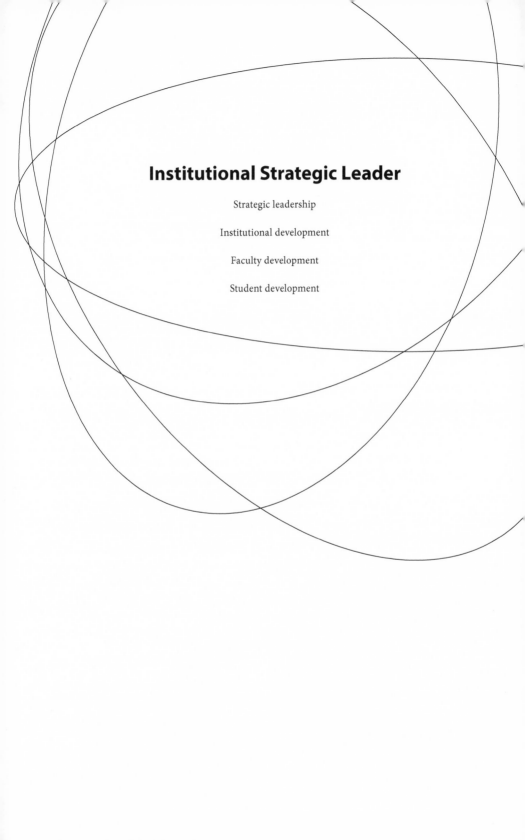

Institutional Strategic Leader

Strategic leadership

Institutional development

Faculty development

Student development

Chapter 1: Institutional Strategic Leader

Nancy Mathias and Betsy Banks

The increasing significance of community engagement to a higher education institution requires an institutional strategic leader. We define institutional strategic leader as the person who provides the vision, knowledge, skills, and relationships to align resources and help the institution achieve its goals for community engagement, living up to its ideals. As an institutional strategic leader, the community engagement professional must work within and across the unique and often "siloed" cultures of faculty, staff, students, and community to communicate and unite these stakeholders to work toward a common purpose that capitalizes on the unique strengths of each partner and the institution itself. To navigate these tasks effectively, the community engagement professional must develop and use a diverse skill set, which includes expertise in:

Strategic leadership

Institutional development

Faculty development

Student development

Strategic Leadership

It is easy for us to feel pulled in too many directions by multiple and sometimes-competing stakeholders; be drawn to quick, visible, feel-good volunteer events; get caught up in day-to-day tasks and issues; and often feel at the end of the day as though the opportunity for real community impact and student learning is slipping away. Effective strategic leadership is key to moving an organization forward by focusing on a few critical priorities and not trying to be everything to everyone. It requires a real desire and ability to facilitate change to improve an organization and the way it works. It requires vision, discipline, and focus, as well as strengthening skills and building relationships. This is not an easy task.

As strategic leaders, we can capitalize on the institution's widely held value of community engagement and service. We must build relationships to harness the power of stakeholders at all levels of the institution to envision a common purpose and a plan that moves the organization forward with clear goals, measures, and ongoing accountability. Strategic leadership uses intentional plans to connect and align service programs with the institution's mission and the evolving needs of the community. It also builds capacity for faculty and service coordinators to lead effective and sustainable service programs to expand the reach of the service experience to more students. Strategic leadership makes service impacts visible through regular communication with stakeholders about progress, successes, and challenges to build confidence and ongoing support.

How do you become a strategic leader? First, assess and expand your leadership knowledge, skills, and development. The framework outlined in *Professional Competency Areas for Student Affairs Practitioners* (American College Personnel Association, 2010) describes leadership competencies that may point you in a helpful direction. It may take a little more study, though, to get a better understanding of what it means to be a strategic leader. The best way may be to find an effective strategic leader in your own backyard and learn from him or her. Scan your campus for department leaders who articulate few, but important, goals and then use clear metrics that show results, not just activities. Seek out and partner with business faculty who teach "lean" thinking and tools such as dashboards, standard work processes, and pull systems for improving strategic thinking, efficiency, and accountability. Create a learning community (on campus or electronically) by drawing together colleagues who are interested in reading, discussing, and experimenting with strategic leadership.

Felten, Bauman, Kheriaty, and Taylor (2013) present ideas for building transformative mentoring communities in higher education. Books by Pascal Dennis, Robert O. Martichenko, and Patrick Lencioni may be good resources for exploring and developing the strategic skills used most commonly in the business and health sectors, and they are just starting to be used in higher education. Look for community experts in the nonprofit or consulting sectors who can recommend local training or coaching resources. The art and science of strategic leadership takes years to develop; requires committed team members for ongoing growth; and can develop more quickly with a good coach, mentor, or conversation partners to encourage and support you in this challenging personal and professional work.

Institutional Development

Many higher education institutions want to see more of their students engaged in high-quality service-learning experiences to fulfill their own mission. Even more broadly, an institution may choose to align its community engagement work with civic and democratic principles of higher education (The National Task Force on Civic Learning and Democratic Engagement, 2012). In either case, this often means expanding, deepening, and strengthening our service and engagement programs or "institutionalizing" service so it is systematically built into our students' college experience in and out of the classroom. By engaging the institution's leadership, key champions, and stakeholders, we can achieve common goals of increased student learning, satisfaction, and retention, while enhancing community partnerships. There are many good resources to explain and assess the process of the institutionalization of service-learning on campus, such as the "Self-Assessment Rubric for Institutionalizing Service Learning in Higher Education" (Furco, 2002) and resources that are listed in the resource section. But here we will look at a few skills we can use to move this process forward.

As institutional leaders, we focus on an ever-widening circle of influence, beginning at the service and engagement program level, moving to the department or division level, and eventually expanding to the institutional level. Start by learning about your institution's leadership, their priorities, and ways that service can benefit those areas. Then identify, articulate, model, and support best practices for engagement and service-learning programs as you work with faculty, staff, and students to strengthen and build sustainability for these programs. Find champions to lead the development and implementation of service-learning and civic engagement in areas in which you may be less familiar. Join committees where you can work with campus stakeholders.

Often a community engagement center or professional can spearhead an application process for service recognition, such as the President's Higher Education Community Service Honor Roll or the Carnegie Elective Classification for Community Engagement. These team efforts can bring a variety of constituents to the table and generate valuable insight and discussion around your campus's community involvement. You might consider establishing a service-learning committee with representatives from across campus to provide feedback to you and your center, engage in dialogue around engagement, and work on initiatives they deem priorities for professional development and institutionalization.

At the department or division level, we suggest you work collaboratively with students, faculty, and staff toward common goals and provide the training and feedback needed to continually improve and report on engagement outcomes for students and the community. Become familiar with any of your existing institutional research based on campus-wide student surveys, such as the National Survey of Student Engagement or the Higher Education Research Institute College Senior Survey, that can show benefits of community engagement on student learning outcomes. Look for evidence on community impact from your accreditation reports or develop and use your own community surveys to show community impact (Gelmon, 2001). Also seek reports or develop tools to show how service impacts college priority areas, such as retention or college rankings. As other chapters in this resource suggest, sharing stories with the president, other campus leaders, and community partners can be a strategic way to move your work forward.

At the campus/community level, we engage in strategic work with the institution's president and administrative leaders, key institutional committees, and key community partners that have the potential to impact the future and reputation of the institution nationally and even internationally. At this level we might make a case for funding a faculty service-learning chair, a service program, or a naming gift for a center as a way of moving institutional priorities forward to increase visibility, sustainability, and impact of service-learning. Institutions with centers can lead to greater institutionalization of service-learning (Bringle & Hatcher, 2000).

Depending on the size and type of institution, you will have different challenges when leading from the bottom, middle, or top of the organization. No matter if you are a service coordinator, director, associate provost, or chief community engagement officer, you must be strategic in engaging the entire institution to develop, fund, and implement community-based learning experiences and begin or strengthen the campus/community partnerships. This will lead to the positive transformations we hope to have.

Faculty Development

Faculty development is a critical component to advancing community engagement across the campus. Key skills and strategies you can develop to support faculty to incorporate service-learning into courses include:

Understanding the climate and culture of your institution's faculty

Facilitating opportunities for faculty to enhance their engagement skills

Building credibility in learning theory and course design

As an entry point, you can begin to understand the culture(s) of your institution's faculty, their familiarity with engaged pedagogy, what barriers they may face in getting involved in community-based work, and how you can make engagement more accessible. Review your institution's faculty handbook, meet with department chairs, and attend a departmental faculty meeting. With a better understanding of faculty priorities and goals, you can demonstrate how community engagement aligns with those goals. Mundy (2004) notes that increasing faculty knowledge and perceptions of service-learning increases the likelihood of them participating in service-learning. You must be able to demonstrate to faculty members how service-learning can be used as a pedagogical tool to meet their educational goals and enhance their students' learning to meet the objectives of a particular course.

There are a variety of ways to provide formal faculty development opportunities to help them understand and implement service-learning. Clayton and O'Steen (2010) outline a continuum of approaches to faculty development that range from a 30-minute presentation at a departmental meeting to a full-day immersion to a semester-long workshop series. They emphasize the importance of meeting faculty members where they are and supporting them, collaborating with them, and continuing to learn with them. In addition to Clayton and O'Steen's work on faculty development, resources such as Campus Compact's (2003) *Introduction to Service-Learning Toolkit: Readings and Resources for Faculty* can provide ideas and information as you design faculty development opportunities.

To effectively assist faculty on academic courses, you need to build your skills as an instructional coach. Participate in workshops offered by your institution to promote faculty excellence in teaching, curriculum design, and learning theory. Become familiar with syllabus construction and models of effective service-learning courses through resources such as Heffernan's (2001) *Fundamentals of Service-Learning Course Construction* and Campus Compact (www.compact.org), which maintains an online syllabus bank of service-learning courses across the disciplines. If the opportunity is available, teaching or co-teaching a course can give you valuable insight into the challenges faculty face with course design, assignment creation, assessment, semester pacing, student motivation, etc. This knowledge will strengthen the relevance of your faculty coaching and build collegial trust in your expertise.

By providing professional development opportunities for faculty, you are not only enhancing faculty skills and access to your center's resources, but you are also building allies for community engagement across your campus. Invite faculty for coffee to discuss their needs and how your center can assist, share compelling examples of community-engaged courses, and ask if there are ways your center can help advance their goals for community engagement. This strategy is sometimes referred to as "friendraising," or cultivating personal relationships through face-to-face interactions (Jamison, 2011). In the digital age, "friendraising" may seem unnecessary, but taking the time and effort to connect with key campus partners can help advance the institutionalization of your program.

Student Development

Working with students as colleagues, leaders, and developers of service programs can contribute dramatically to the effectiveness and reach of your community engagement office. Zlotkowski, Longo, and Williams (2006) describe three specific rationales for engaging students as colleagues in our service work: as an instrumental way to expand office staff, to more fully engage and empower students, and to capitalize on the gifts brought by this new generation of students. Exceptional student engagement leaders can help shape the direction of service on campus, create model programs that contribute to positive and sustainable community change, and add to the national conversation on service and civic engagement.

Developing these exceptional student leaders requires us to have another set of skills. Minimally, we should be knowledgeable about student development theory and practice, especially as they relate to service and leadership development (American College Personnel Association, 2010). Some helpful student development models to consider may be the Active Citizen Continuum (Break Away), the Leadership Identity Development model (Komives, Longerbeam, Owen, Mainella, & Osteen, 2006), and the Social Change Model of Leadership Development (Higher Education Research Institute, 1996). We should use best practices and train and support students to employ them (Howard, 2001). With more experience, we can partner with other student development professionals to embed service across campus in programs such as new-student orientation, first-year experience, living-learning communities, student clubs and organizations, interfaith understanding, and diversity initiatives. We can partner with faculty to prepare students to serve as course assistants, co-researchers and engaged scholars, community partner liaisons and site supervisors, leaders in training and reflection, and even bridges between academic and student affairs (Zlotkowski et al., 2006).

Students can connect institutions to national organizations where they may gain deeper, more specialized service training and a national perspective on issues they care about through programs such as Alternative Break Citizenship Schools (Break Away), Change Leaders (OxFam), civic reflection training (Center for Civic Reflection), and LeaderShape. By bringing their learning from these national experiences back to campus intentionally and with staff support, students can raise the quality of service experiences across campus in often-surprising ways with multiplying effects. Working together, students, faculty, staff, and community partners can join the national movement for re-imagining the role of higher education in educating citizens and building communities.

Conclusion

It is an exciting time in higher education, with increasing public concern for evidence that the rising cost of tuition is a good investment and the demand that higher education lives out its mandate to benefit the public good. Service-learning can be a part of the response to these concerns when it is developed thoughtfully and strategically through excellent institutional leadership. As effective community engagement professionals, we must work with multiple stakeholders to build relationships and programs. By providing professional development opportunities for faculty to build skills in implementing service-learning courses and student development programs that enhance leadership skills in community-based work, we play an important role in helping our institutions advance institutionalization of community engagement on our campuses.

Appendix 1A: Case Studies From the Field

Case Study 1: Lessons in Developing an Office of Service-Learning // Julia M. Yakovich

Over the years, I have learned important lessons about building an office of service-learning that anyone can use in his or her position:

Be the example of service-learning. Believe in modeling and being the change, especially when everyone around you is new to service-learning. Following through on even the smallest act is important. I offered programs, workshops, alternative spring breaks, internships, work-study opportunities, and especially service-learning courses. Each followed service-learning models to strategically create a uniform message to stakeholders.

Reciprocal relationships are essential; create allies. It was important to me to find the group of faculty and community partners who had bought into service-learning and learn from them. With faculty, especially in the beginning, you will learn about this pedagogy together. As you increase your knowledge base, you can help guide them toward service-learning to be sure their courses meet criteria. With community partners, develop projects together with faculty. Manage realistic expectations of the partnership, in addition to ensuring both sides will benefit. Do your best to keep all parties satisfied with the experience.

Community partners or faculty: Who comes first? It will be difficult to answer what came first, the chicken or the egg? Start with your personal contacts. The simple and complicated answer is you have to work with both faculty and community partners simultaneously. Get to know faculty members and community partners and build quality relationships. Do not make promises you cannot keep and maintain realistic expectations. If you do make promises, work really hard to see them through.

Learn the landscape, meet the people. Become familiar with all areas of the institution because service-learning can be relevant anywhere. If you can teach a class, teach. If you can be part of the advising staff, do it. Get to know the students through your student government and leadership programs.

The office/initiative needs a champion. A champion is someone in upper-level administration committed to raising the profile of service-learning. This individual will help you push service-learning toward institutionalizing course designation, promotion and tenure processes, and engaged scholarship. All are vital to the progress and value of service-learning.

In developing an office of service-learning, it is important to be patient, flexible, adaptable, diverse, encouraging, confident, and positive. You must have a vision. Service-learning is unlike anything else at your institution. Take it a little at a time, learn from your challenges, and be the best representative of service-learning there is on campus.

Case Study 2: Stakeholder Input: A Critical Ingredient to Program Success and Sustainability // Maggie Baker

From conceptualizing a program to training students, staff, and faculty to evaluating programs and initiatives, I have found stakeholder input, via ongoing collaborative efforts, to be a critical ingredient to success. My career as a community engagement professional, which began in 1998, has involved building curricular and co-curricular programs at two small private institutions in the Midwest, both of which have received national recognition for their service programs. When establishing the programs, I collected feedback from multiple constituents to ensure the foundations were built for a future that could include the empowerment of many to engage in, lead, and champion service in sustainable ways.

Examples of this strategy have included:

- Interviewing faculty to understand what they are looking for in a program and how it ties to their scholarship, research, and personal interests. During the first months of building a co-curricular program at Buena Vista University in 1998, I interviewed at least 80% of faculty members to learn more about their interests and to gain insight into what types of partnerships with nonprofits would most effectively support their efforts to integrate service learning into their future courses. This strategy guided the process of building partnerships that, though primarily focused on immediately supporting co-curricular service, had the potential to support curricular service in the future.

- Collaborating with colleagues in student development to establish a strategy to leverage AmeriCorps in support of co-curricular service. In the early stages of implementing an AmeriCorps program at Loras College, I worked closely with the director of student life to determine how we could most effectively leverage the program to support leaders of student organizations primarily focused on serving the community. The program was piloted by helping leaders build and sustain volunteer capacity in the popular dance marathon organization that is affiliated with the Children's Miracle Network. This was achieved by strengthening the organization's focus on engaging its peers in serving and learning about the social issues of family support for children with serious health conditions and access to affordable health care. The college has now successfully scaled out this approach to include two more student organizations focused on serving and learning in the areas of supporting self-determination of individuals with intellectual disabilities and raising awareness about mental health.

- Investing time and effort with community partner organizations to define, on a case-by-case basis, what constitutes a reciprocal partnership to them. Loras College has supported an approach to building strategic community partnerships. It has involved a time-consuming process of working with a few nonprofit organizations to build capacity to support ongoing service. In partnership with these organizations, we have been able to leverage Iowa Campus Compact VISTA members to determine what the organizations need to do to help them more effectively use volunteers. Once capacity for volunteer management has been built, each organization is then poised to understand and measure how citizens (a portion of whom are involved in curricular and co-curricular service at institutions of higher education) are serving with them to impact a social issue, such as poverty or making the arts more accessible to all citizens.

Appendix 1B: Reflection Questions

Novice Professionals

- How can I connect our campus mission/goals to national benchmarks, standards, and resources to build excitement and support for service-learning work?

- What personal areas do I need to develop to become a stronger leader? Advocate? Educator?

- What are my personal and professional motivations for working in this field?

- How can an advisory board help us achieve our goals by complementing and developing our staff's skills and connecting us to stakeholders?

Intermediate Professionals

- What are our stakeholders' top three priorities for our program that will allow our staff to focus on these and say no (or not now) to other things?

- Which on-campus leaders do I need to connect with to help them better understand our community engagement programs?

- Which community leaders do I need to connect with to help them better understand our community engagement programs?

- What sections of our institution's strategic plan connect to community engagement, and how can I articulate our department's contribution to those sections?

- What professional development opportunities do I need to take advantage of to become a stronger leader? Advocate? Educator?

Advanced Professionals

- How do I connect with mentors in the national arena to continue to grow in my profession and contribute to the field?

- What committees can I serve on to create stronger connections to institutional leaders and have an influence on institutional investment in community engagement?

- What can I uniquely contribute to this field as a community engagement professional?

- How can I show our programs' successes and improvements in a simple annual report?

About the Authors and Contributors

Maggie Baker has served as service-learning coordinator at Loras College since August 2006. She has developed the institutional and community infrastructure necessary to support academically embedded community-based learning and reciprocal, strategic partnerships. Prior to her work at Loras, Maggie was the first director of community service and internships at Buena Vista University. She received her B.S. in family and consumer sciences from the University of Arizona and her M.A. in social sciences from the Universiteit van Amsterdam in the Netherlands.

Betsy Banks serves as director of the Center for Civic Engagement & Learning (CCEL) at Case Western Reserve University (CWRU). CCEL provides and supports opportunities for direct community service, service-learning, and collective action, while promoting civic awareness and leadership. Betsy received her undergraduate degree from Bowdoin College and a master's degree from Miami University. Before arriving at CWRU in 1998, she led wilderness service programs in Yellowstone and Everglades national parks and worked in conservation and volunteer management with The Nature Conservancy in Maine, California, and Kentucky.

Nancy Mathias serves as director for the Sturzl Center for Community Service and Learning at St. Norbert College. She joined the college in 1990, working in the areas of experiential education, leadership development, and service-learning programs. She helped establish the Sturzl Center in 2010 and continues to support the institutionalization of service-learning and community engagement at the college. She earned her master's degree in education from Cardinal Stritch University.

Julia Mastronardi Yakovich is the director of service-learning for the University of Connecticut. Julia has spent her career working within the not-for-profit and government sectors. She strives to incorporate and share resources to produce the best outcomes for stakeholders she serves: students, faculty, and community partners. Julia earned her B.A.

in business and communications from Regis College, Weston, and an M.A. and a master's of public administration from the University of Connecticut. Since 2007, she has been developing the Office of Service-Learning at UConn, combining her passion for community, program development, and academics.

References

American College Personnel Association and National Association of Student Personnel Administrators. (2010). *Professional competency areas for student affairs professionals* Washington, DC: American College Personnel Association and National Association of Student Personnel Administrators.

Bringle, R.G., & Hatcher, J.A. (2000). Institutionalization of service learning in higher education. *Journal of Higher Education, 71*, 273-290.

Clayton, P. H., & O'Steen, B. (2010). Working with faculty: Designing customized developmental strategies. In B. Jacoby & P. Mutascio (Eds.), *Looking in reaching out: A reflective guide for community service-learning professionals* (pp. 95-135). Boston, MA: Campus Compact.

Felten, P., Bauman, H.D.L., Kheriaty, A., & Taylor, E. (2013). *Transformative conversations: A guide to mentoring communities among colleagues in higher education.* San Francisco, CA: Josey-Bass

Furco, A. (2002). *Self-assessment rubric for the institutionalization of service-learning in higher education.* Providence, RI: Campus Compact.

Furco, A., & Holland, B. (2004). Institutionalizing service-learning in higher education: Issues and strategies for chief academic officers. In M. Langseth & S. Dillon (Eds.), *Public work and the academy: An academic administrator's guide to civic engagement and service learning*. Bolton, MA: Anker Publishing Company.

Gelmon, S. B. (2001). *Assessing service-learning and civic engagement: Principles and techniques*. Providence, RI: Campus Compact, Brown University.

Heffernan, K. (2001). *Fundamentals of service-learning course construction*. Providence, RI: Campus Compact, Brown University.

Higher Education Research Institute (1996). *A social change model of leadership development: Guidebook, version III*. University of California, Los Angeles. Retrieved from http://www.heri.ucla.edu/PDFs/pubs/ASocialChangeModelofLeadershipDevelopment.pdf

Howard, J. (2001, Summer). Principles of good practice for service-learning pedagogy. *Michigan Journal of Community Service-Learning*, Summer 2001, 16-19.

Jacoby, B., & Mutascio, P. (Eds.). (2010). *Looking in reaching out: A reflective guide for community service-learning professionals*. Boston, MA: Campus Compact.

Jamison, J. (2011). Becoming an advocate. In M. Eisenhauer, N. Marthakis, J. Jamison, & M. Mattson (Eds.), *Charting the course for service-learning: From curriculum considerations to advocacy-A faculty development workbook* (151-165). Indianapolis, IN: Indiana Campus Compact.

Campus Compact. (2003). *Introduction to service-learning toolkit: Readings and resources for faculty* (2nd ed.). Providence, RI: Campus Compact, Brown University.

Komives, S. R., Longerbeam, S. D., Owen, J. E., Mainella, F. C., & Osteen, L. (2006). A leadership identity development model: Applications from a grounded theory. *Journal of College Student Development, 47*(4), 401-418.

The National Task Force on Civic Learning and Democratic Engagement. (2012). *A crucible moment: College learning and democracy's future*. Washington, DC: Association of American Colleges and Universities. Retrieved from http://www.aacu.org/civic_learning/crucible/http://www.aacu.org/civic_learning/crucible/

Munday, M. E. (2004). Faculty engagement in service-learning: Individual and organizational factors at distinct institutional types. In M. Welch & S. H. Billig (Eds.), *New perspectives in service-learning: Research to advance the field*, 169-193. Greenwich, CT: Information Age Publishing.

Zlotkowski, E. A., Longo, N. V., & Williams, J. R. (Eds.). (2006). *Students as colleagues: Expanding the circle of service-learning leadership*. Providence, RI: Campus Compact, Brown University.

Critical Response: Institutional Strategic Leader

Andrew Seligsohn, Ph.D., President, Campus Compact

I found myself sitting across the table from our brand-new dean of arts and sciences during her first week on the job. I had been leading our campus civic engagement efforts for a little more than a year, and I was excited to have the opportunity to pitch this creative and energetic new colleague on my ideas for integrating civic engagement more deeply into the academic program. I knew I needed her help. As at many institutions, the money on our campus was mostly in the hands of the deans. Perhaps more importantly, the deans are the leaders of their faculties, and the faculties control curricula, tenure standards, and on-the-ground pedagogy. With the active support of the new arts and sciences dean, I had a pretty good shot at achieving success in advancing civic engagement on our campus. Without it, my job was going to be much harder.

As you would imagine, I was prepared. While I wanted to share my broad agenda with the dean to win her overall support, my primary goal was for her to embrace a plan I had developed for a summer civic engagement faculty development seminar. The proposal was a thing of beauty. I had begun crafting it while at a previous institution, where I had not had the opportunity to bring the plan to fruition. I did not want that to happen again.

The dean, an accomplished and experienced higher education leader, was skeptical. She thought it unlikely that faculty at a research university would dedicate a substantial portion of the summer to such a seminar, even with a financial incentive. She proposed, instead, a workshop in January just before the start of the spring semester. I really, really liked my own plan. And just like that, I told the dean I thought her idea was great and moved the discussion to how we could work together to make it happen. In the end, we built a Civic Engagement Faculty Fellows Program that involved a two-day intensive workshop in January and follow-up sessions throughout the spring semester. All faculty fellows built new syllabi, which, over just a few years, had a dramatic impact on the curriculum. And we built a cohort of faculty members personally connected to the overall civic engagement agenda.

It's not the case that everything I did at Rutgers-Camden worked out as well, but the origin of our Faculty Fellows Program calls to mind a few lessons about what it takes to succeed as an institutional strategic leader. First, understand your own goals. I liked my proposal, but my proposal was a vehicle for the larger purposes of catalyzing curricular change and building faculty investment in civic engagement. Your goals are, of course, the substance of your strategy. It makes sense for them to be big and ambitious, which means there are likely to be various plausible routes for achieving them. Second, remember you are unlikely to achieve anything significant using only resources directly under your control. You will need other people's money, other people's expertise, and other people's relationships. Third, most people do not want to sit and listen to you tell them why they should want what you want. But most people do like to be asked what they want, and they are likely to be open to exploring the possibility of shaping plans around the intersection between their goals and yours. Finally, remember that others may actually have things to teach you. When you decide to reshape a plan, it may simply be a compromise to get someone to come on board. But it may also be that the other person understands something you do not. Community engagement professionals talk a lot about building mutually respectful partnerships with our neighbors outside our institutions. It's important to do the same thing with our campus colleagues.

I have learned these lessons over time—frequently through false starts and outright failures—as the scope of my responsibility has expanded. Some of that expansion has been the result of formal changes in my role (from center staff member to director of civic engagement to associate chancellor for civic engagement to president of Campus Compact). But my responsibilities also expanded because I recognized the opportunity to act as an institutional strategic leader. As director of civic engagement, I decided I could make my university better by seeing myself not merely as the leader of a department, but as an institutional leader facilitating collaboration among campus units and between campus units and communities. We speak of opportunities presenting themselves, but in my experience, what really happens is opportunities meet us halfway. If we step forward, presenting ourselves as leaders dedicated to the core purposes of colleges and universities, we may find that others take that at face value and work with us to change our institutions and our communities for the better.

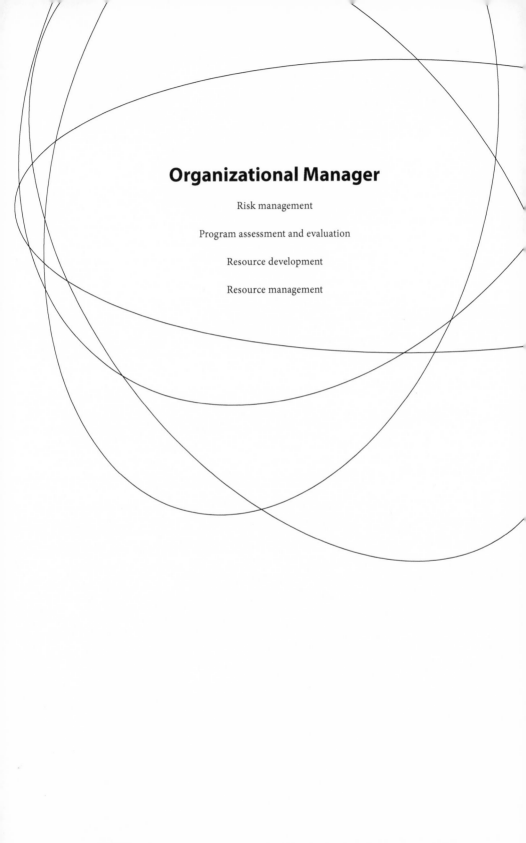

Organizational Manager

Risk management

Program assessment and evaluation

Resource development

Resource management

Chapter 2: Organizational Manager

Ashley Farmer-Hanson

Every institution has the assessment guru, the person who knows everything you want to know about risk management and the person who can manage five programs at one time. This chapter will focus on the organizational manager as a person who performs all these roles at once. We define the organizational manager as the person who is highly skilled in assessment; resource development; and organizational management, which includes human resources, risk management, and program management. They juggle many roles and have a wide variety of knowledge bases that serve their institution and community. Being a strong organizational manager requires practicality and an ability to tackle new tasks quickly.

The organizational manager oversees the work of civic and community engagement on a campus. He or she focuses on many aspects of program management, but this chapter covers a few particular competencies and resources for further information. These four areas are important, particularly because they are key aspects of keeping a department running and can protect the university from litigation:

Risk management

Program assessment and evaluation

Resource development

Resource management

Risk Management

Community engagement professionals should be well-versed in institutional policies and procedures related to risk management. Additional information on risk management and liability can be found on the National Service-Learning Clearinghouse website (www.servicelearning.org). Risk management is very important in community work because a large part of the work students do is off campus. Practitioners must create a safe and educational environment for both students and community partners. Risk management must be considered in everything we do, which can be a challenge. Those who understand this area will shine, while those who do not will struggle and put their institution at risk for litigation. Risk management is essentially taking the "proactive steps to minimize accidental injury and/or loss" (Arizona State University, n.d.). According to the Arizona State University Student Risk Management webpage, risk management is something that can be addressed in five steps:

Identify *potential risks*

Evaluate *the risks and any consequences of the risks*

Determine *the most effective way to mitigate each risk*

Implement *a plan to eliminate or mitigate the risks and educate others*

Assess *the event or service activity to ensure all risks were addressed*

This all can be done by visiting the service sites and by providing orientation and training to your students. Just like with other areas, communication is vital, and finding a community of support can assist in this area. Having conversations with your institutional risk management director to understand campus policies is key to being successful. The next step is sharing this information with nonprofit partners and finding out about their needs. Through these conversations, you not only educate one another, you also build community and keep everyone safe. Another good technique is to reach out to other professionals in your state or at similar institutions to learn more about their approaches and find model policies and procedures.

Program Assessment & Evaluation

An organizational manager knows how to fully evaluate a program, assess results, and report impacts to make improvements, and he or she has a deep understanding of the variety of assessment and evaluation tools available to undertake these tasks. An organizational manager has the skill set to assess and evaluate programs and a good understanding of the value of both (see Table 2.1). Evaluation can be difficult because most organizational managers feel as if they are doing work that is of value and merit, but until they conduct an evaluation of their programs, they will

Table 2.1
Evaluation vs. Assessment

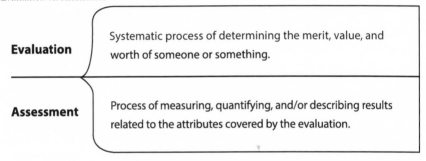

Evaluation	Systematic process of determining the merit, value, and worth of someone or something.
Assessment	Process of measuring, quantifying, and/or describing results related to the attributes covered by the evaluation.

American Evaluators Association, 2014

not fully see and be able to prove that value. A program should first be assessed and then evaluated for its effectiveness. Through the assessment process, if we learn that the program is not meeting learning outcomes, that is when it should be evaluated to see what changes can be made. As an organizational manager, you should have a knowledge base of institution-level assessment tools and standards, such as the "Self-Assessment Rubric for the Institutionalization of Service-Learning in Higher Education" (Furco, 2002), American Association of Colleges and Universities' "Civic Engagement Value Rubric," and the Council for the Advancement of Standards (CAS) in Higher Education. These tools will help you benchmark your own activities.

In community engagement, individuals should also be familiar with means of assessing and promoting their programs through award and recognition programs, such as the President's Higher Education Community Service Honor Roll and the Carnegie Elective Classification in Community Engagement. For the U.S. Department of Education and many accrediting bodies, program assessment should demonstrate that student learning outcomes are being met and that students are receiving a quality learning experience (U.S. Department of Education, n.d.). Effective program evaluation and student learning assessment will help community engagement professionals ensure that best practices are in place for our institutions to build capacity with our community partners, encourage community development, and advance student learning (Publow, 2010).

Organizational managers should also have skills to assess campus and local community needs and meet those needs through educational and direct programming. Needs assessments are vital to ensuring that all parties' goals are met (Publow, 2010). Well-designed community needs assessments ensure that community partner voices are included in the process and help create successful capacity building endeavors. Without the voices of community partners, community goals and missions may not be met. Connecting community needs with student learning outcomes will ensure that students learn from the experience and that the activity will meet the needs of a community partner and work toward impacting a community-identified issue.

Resource Development

A successful organizational manager should have the ability to recognize areas of growth within departments and develop and implement a fundraising plan to ensure programs are sustainable over time. Strategic fundraising requires developing strong proposals that articulate for potential funders what they would be supporting, what support is needed, and what the outcomes will be. Professionals need to develop a strong foundation in a variety of fundraising methods, including grant seeking and proposal writing, student-led fundraising efforts, and organizing fundraising events. Professionals need to be able to use institutional resources by developing strategic partnerships with development staff and other leaders in campus fundraising efforts.

Campus development offices have established resources, funding networks, and, typically, several years of experience and training. By developing an understanding of the university's funding goals and communicating your office needs, you can have a plan to move forward and tackle the project together. Often, development offices not only have access to grants, endowments, and donor networks, they also have access to training opportunities. Through an established relationship, a coordinated training session for staff and students could assist with building a resource network. These partnerships can help to build efforts into campus fundraising through alumni, major donors, corporate sponsors, and others, and they can create sustainable funding sources, such as endowments. Finally, to continue to receive funding, professionals need to build systems for strong grants management and reporting to demonstrate to funders the impact of their contributions and the need for ongoing support.

Resource Management

One framework that may be helpful in thinking about how to be a successful organizational manager is a model developed by Bolman and Deal (2008) (see Table 2.2). In this framework, individuals should have the ability to manage an organization from structural, political, symbolic, and human resource frames of reference. Understanding the structural framework of an organization is important because there are institutional rules—written or underlying—that have an impact on the organization. The political framework focuses on power, conflict, and advocacy. A good professional will have the ability to recognize in various situations who is perceived to have power, how to advocate for those who do not, and how to balance it all internally and externally. The symbolic framework may be the most difficult for a new manager.

Table 2.2
Resource Framework

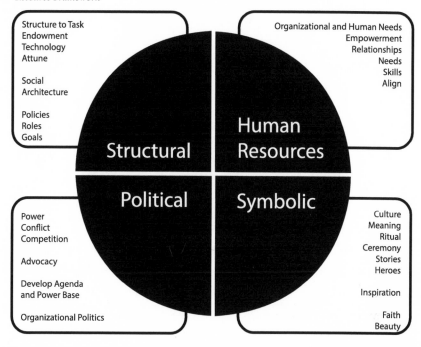

Structural	Human Resources
Structure to Task Endowment Technology Attune Social Architecture Policies Roles Goals	Organizational and Human Needs Empowerment Relationships Needs Skills Align
Political	**Symbolic**
Power Conflict Competition Advocacy Develop Agenda and Power Base Organizational Politics	Culture Meaning Ritual Ceremony Stories Heroes Inspiration Faith Beauty

Bolman & Deal, 2008

This framework focuses on making meaning of the institutional culture, developing an understanding of rituals, and interpreting them.

Structural, political, and symbolic skills are important when managing an organization; however, human resource management is imperative. Even if you do not directly supervise staff, you are likely to use student workers, volunteers, or others to help accomplish goals. To do this well, organizational managers should have knowledge of evaluation and motivation theories in which to ground their daily efforts to maximize this critical resource. For example, knowledge in something similar to Maslow's hierarchy of needs will assist in understanding how to continually motivate employees to be committed to the task and job at hand (Bolman & Deal, 2008). If employees' basic needs are not being met, then they will not be productive and will not reach individual or professional goals. Professionals should be very familiar with their institution's policies and procedures and resources available to assist in human resource issues. Organizational managers also need to have the ability to guide the professional development of their staff and volunteers and help them reach their full potential. Using these frames helps develop good relationships and build a better environment in which to learn and work.

Conclusion

Developing the skills and knowledge needed in all of these areas can be a challenge for any one individual. Professionals need to look at their strengths and identify gaps in skills and knowledge to design professional development programs and lean on others to help shore up certain areas. Organizational management is an area in particular where other institutional partners, such as research and assessment staff, development staff, legal teams, and human resources staff, are generally available and should be considered and cultivated.

Appendix 2A: Case Studies From the Field

Case Study 1: Risk Management

After a new office for community engagement was established at a small liberal arts university in the Midwest, it was discovered the institution was sending student service-learning participants into the community without a signed liability waiver, therefore putting the institution at a high risk for liability.

It was recognized that a process was needed to avoid continued risk. The staff person met with the director of the career center to determine what the institution was using for practicum, internship, and student teaching liability. It was determined that what the career center office had been using was insufficient and needed to be updated.

Both offices worked together to gather samples of liability/risk management procedures from similar institutions in the state. They used these samples as they developed a draft. After developing the first draft, the directors worked with the institution's attorney to determine if they were adequately covering the school's risk. Once the institution's attorney approved the liability waiver, it was shared with all faculty and staff and implemented in all experiential learning programs at the university.

Case Study 2: Program Development and Evaluation With Students

A program manager at a small private college in a town of fewer than 10,000 can sometimes find it difficult to identify meaningful places and programs where students can serve. Dr. Ashley Farmer-Hanson does this through a student-led organization, Student M.O.V.E. (Mobilize, Outreach, and Volunteer Efforts). This student-led board is made up of a president and nine vice presidents. Sometimes two students serve as co-vice presidents if a role or goals for that year are large. Roles include:

marketing and advertisement, communication, special events, alternative events, hours and competition, community relations, alternative spring breaks, organization relations, recruitment, and retention. This student board conducts a needs assessment on campus and within the local community. The vice presidents' roles are to design programing efforts based on those needs.

For example, a local nonprofit frequently needs volunteers to assist with food packaging and distribution to community members in need. Student M.O.V.E. members help recruit volunteers, train them for risk management purposes, assess learning outcomes, host events to thank them, and then encourage them to log their service hours. Through marketing and communications, other students are made aware of events via social media and newsletters. The students also identified that not all the student volunteers understand the underlying issues of poverty and hunger. M.O.V.E. students design events not only to educate about the need in the local community, but also on other efforts to address the underlying issues found in the community needs assessment.

It is the professional's role to conduct risk management and assess the program, teach the students those skills, and explain to them why it is important. The challenge with student-led organizations is that every year there is a new group of leaders that works with the community agencies. This can be a hindrance to a nonprofit if new people are continually coming in and out of their agency, which must then invest time doing the same training it did in previous years. In higher education, this is something most people are used to, but finding nonprofits that are understanding and willing to serve as co-educators can be a challenge if not done right.

Appendix 2B: Reflection Questions

Novice Professionals

- What is our risk management plan, and what is the institution's stance on liability and coverage?

- Who on campus can assist me with assessment and evaluation? Who has the historical information and can help develop a baseline understanding of what is taking place?

- What are the current needs of the community, and how can we meet them?

- What are my current funding sources, and how can I leverage them? What small grants are available in the local community that would support my efforts?

- What is my role at the institution and within the community as an organizational manager?

Intermediate Professionals

- What are our current areas of risk on campus and at service sites? Who on campus can field questions about our risk management policy?

- What assessment tool is best for my institution? What other ways can I assess my institution and the programs that I manage? How do I use assessment information? How can I better close the loop and report data and stories back to students, community partners, donors, administration officials, policy leaders, and others?

- What are the current needs of faculty, staff, and students? How can I assess these needs and develop programing efforts around them?

- Which programs are successful, and which programs could be advanced with additional funding sources? What funding sources (grants, endowments, small event fund-raisers) would be best for the projects I have?

- As a department, how do community service-learning efforts fit into the bigger picture of the campus community? What is our role in the local and global community? How can we keep this at the center of what we do, while maintaining a work-life balance?

Advanced Professionals

- What are the areas of risk management that need to be shared with the campus community prior to service? Where can I post resources on risk management that can be easily accessed?

- How can I use my assessment findings to advance the field of community service-learning? What is the institution doing to advance the field? At what conferences or presentations can I present my findings? To what publications can I submit my findings?

- What tool is best to use to evaluate the staff? What motivational theories do I need to use with each employee to ensure they feel as if this is a supportive, innovative, and comfortable work environment?

- What tools are needed to conduct a community needs assessment? How can I use this to develop a strategic plan that connects to the larger university strategic plan?

- How do I maintain my relationships with donors and foundations? What information do they need to ensure their donation is worth their investment?

- How am I building and maintaining relationships with the various constituents I work with, i.e. faculty, staff, students, and community partners?

- Am I effectively using my capacity in terms of human resources? How am I motivating my employees and volunteers?

About the Authors and Contributors

Ashley Farmer-Hanson serves as the director of civic engagement for Buena Vista University in Storm Lake, Iowa. Ashley is a BVU alumna with a bachelor's degree in elementary education. She also has a master's degree in student affairs administration from the University of Wisconsin La Crosse and a doctorate in education administration: higher education from the University of South Dakota. In addition to her role at BVU, Ashley serves on the Iowa Commission on Volunteer Service. Ashley resides in Storm Lake with her husband, Matt. In her free time, she trains for marathons, spends time with family, and volunteers.

Heidi Pries serves as the director of new-student programs, student involvement, and service learning for Grand View University in Des Moines, Iowa. Heidi earned her B.A. from Grand View University in mass communications. She earned her M.A. in education from the University of Northern Iowa, with an emphasis on higher education and service learning. Prior to working at Grand View, Heidi worked for Wartburg College in Waverly, Iowa. She resides in Grimes, Iowa, with her husband and two sons and enjoys reading, running, and baking.

References

American Evaluators Association. (2014). Retrieved from http://www.eval.org/p/bl/et/ blogid=2&blogaid=4

Arizona State University. (n.d.). Student risk management. Retrieved from http://www.asu.edu/ studentaffairs/risk/what_is_risk_management.htm

Bolman, L., & Deal, T. (2008). *Reframing organizations: Artistry, choice and leadership.* San Francisco, CA: John Wiley & Sons, Inc.

Furco, A. (2002). *Self-assessment rubric for the institutionalization of service-learning in higher education.* Providence, RI: Campus Compact.

Publow, M. (2010). Partnerships: Framework for working together. Retrieved from http:// strengtheningnonprofits.org/resources/guidebooks/Partnerships.pdf

U.S. Department of Education. (n.d.). The database of accredited postsecondary institutions and programs. Retrieved from http://ope.ed.gov/accreditation/

Critical Response: Organizational Manager

Agnieszka Nance, Ph.D., Director, Center for Public Service, Tulane University

Our work in the field of service-learning and community engagement can be challenging—even overwhelming at times. We often find ourselves juggling multiple roles and managing numerous programs at once. While the duties associated with the position of "organizational manager" may seem clear cut—even obvious—the position involves a complex array of responsibilities that go far beyond the seemingly transparent title.

So what does it take to make the position successful and ensure the maximum benefit for our community and our university?

The advice I would give, having served in this role for the past seven years, is that we first make sure we *understand the intricacies* of our programs and the needs of our institutions and communities; then, we can begin to *develop meaningful relationships*. In fact, building partnerships within and outside of campus can and will significantly impact the direction and long-term success of our work. *Engaging campus colleagues* in meaningful dialogue can result in an overall culture change at our institution—one that emphasizes service as integral to a well-rounded education. Similarly, *collaborating with community partners* keeps us in tune with the needs of the community and allows us to serve them in the most meaningful way. To work effectively as an organizational manager, one must *develop a strategic plan and specific action steps* with the support and agreement of the people he or she serves. Focus groups, open discussions, and honest dialogue are vital to securing our constituencies' active participation and support of the larger mission. In every aspect of the daily routine, we need to *keep the bigger picture in mind* and be aware of our constituencies' needs and contributions.

Naturally, it takes time to realize who you are as a manager. You need to reflect on the strengths and weaknesses of your personality and how these qualities influence your work. Question how to ensure that our work is innovative and fresh and find ways to keep our environment supportive and welcoming. Professional development is crucial to our ability to be leaders in the field. No matter how advanced one is in her or his career, the opportunity to reflect on one's efforts and goals and engage in the latest discussion about best practices can have a dramatic effect on a manager's ability to lead staff, students, and supporters.

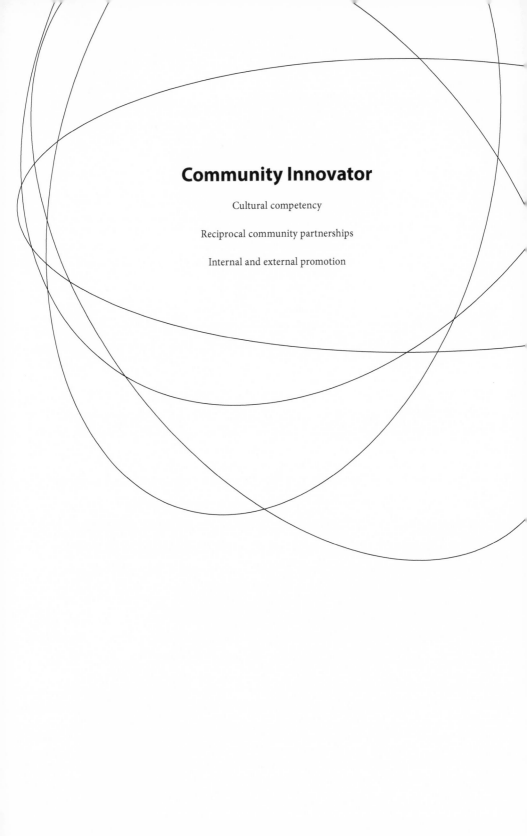

Community Innovator

Cultural competency

Reciprocal community partnerships

Internal and external promotion

Chapter 3: Community Innovator

Maggie Baker and Katie Halcrow

A combined 20 years of experience in the field of civic engagement has reinforced our shared passion and belief that our work should begin and end in our role as a community innovator. This experience has taught us that where the rubber hits the road in civic engagement is through community impact. This is where our institutions collaborate with stakeholders on and off campus to contribute to transforming our communities, and it is where we delight in how our communities transform our institutions. We define a community innovator as the "go to" person skilled in leveraging the human and social capital of an institution of higher education. This is accomplished by building partnerships aimed at pursuing innovative solutions to challenges individuals face.

Building community partnerships and creating opportunities for education and transformation require a specialized skill set. We believe effective practice as a community innovator requires skill-building in three major areas:

Cultural competency

Reciprocal community partnerships

Internal and external promotion

In this chapter, we elaborate on these competency areas and discuss important literatures that have helped us form our identities as community innovators.

Scholars challenged the field to think about how we work with community-based organizations and the cultural implications of the way in which we conceptualize ourselves as partners in a community (Worrall, 2007; Stoecker & Tryon, 2009). Tryon and Stoecker (2007) provided the field with greatly needed standards for building community partnerships for service-learning, while Barbara Jacoby (2003) and associates in their book, *Building Partnerships for Community-Based Learning,* pushed practitioners to delve deeper into the structure of and approach to building community partnerships. Included in this publication is a framework for conceptualizing relationships within campus-community partnerships, encouraging a shared focus on an end goal of transformation within a community (Enos & Morton, 2003).

A focus on transforming communities through the method of collective impact has recently become an important framework and effective guide for the fields of education and criminal justice, making a compelling case for multiple parties in communities to coordinate efforts toward social impact, focused on a common agenda, shared measurement, mutual reinforcing activities, and continuous communication and background support (Kania & Kramer, 2011).

An increasing number of institutions of higher education have also prioritized becoming "anchor institutions" in their communities. These institutions are not limited to just colleges and universities, but they are, as Marausse (2007) points out, institutions so socially embedded in the life and culture of a city, that life in that community without their presence would be unimaginable. The anchor institution movement is contributing to a rich body of scholarly work focused on the impact higher education can make beyond the boundaries of the college campus. The Widener University case study later in this chapter serves as an in-depth look at this model.

Cultural Competency

No task can be more daunting for a new or seasoned professional arriving at a new institution in a new location than becoming as culturally competent as possible in a new community. Acknowledging, understanding, and deferring to members of sub-communities outside the institution, as the true experts, is what we have found to be the wisest and most authentic approach to our work and is an approach supported by multiple scholars in the field (Maurasse, 2001; Bushhouse, 2005; Worrall, 2007; Stoecker & Tryon, 2009).

Each institution of higher education has its own history within the history of the community in which it is located. Becoming familiar and knowledgeable about this history and the implications of it on your work can take time; patience; an open mind; and a desire to seek out ideas, opinions, and information from multiple stakeholders. The public purpose of higher education to educate and train generations to serve others has considerable historical roots ranging from such examples of the land-grant model to historically black colleges and universities, from tribal colleges and universities to urban research university centers and community colleges. Even if the public purpose of your institution is not overtly stated in your mission, Langseth & Plater (2004) points out, "No college or university can be so narrowly focused, so vocationally oriented, or so committed to a certain belief that it does not have an obligation to account for its contribution to sustaining a civil society, contributing to the common good, or improving the human condition through discovery, dissemination, or application of knowledge" (p. 2). Dewey (1916) contended, "Education, in its broadest sense, is the means of this social continuity of life" (p. 3). The concept of "the scholarship of engagement" also challenges institutions to reshape the culture of higher education to focus more on developing partnerships within the community and, as a result, reshape student learning and the professional lives of faculty (Dewey, 1916; Boyer, 1990).

Understanding your institution's cultural journey to realizing its commitment to public purpose within the larger community can be viewed as a marathon, not as a sprint. Learning about multiple versions of both histories and how they are intertwined in the eyes of multiple stakeholders can seem overwhelming at times. We promise a fresh perspective and open mind can be incredible assets to both the institution and community. The field of civic engagement can represent the future hopes and aspirations of a community because our work deals with educating the community's newly minted scholars, professionals, and younger citizens (Battistoni, 2002). Bringing a commitment to collaboration and a focus on shared impact and reciprocal relationships can allow the institution to contribute to building and sustaining incredible partnerships with the community.

Getting started on the task of becoming culturally competent in a new community—or more accurately, set of communities—could involve attending events that immerse you in community dialogue around social issues, such as attending school board, city council, county supervisor meetings, and/or reading archived minutes from such meetings. You could participate in rallies, town hall meetings, citizen action groups, or meetings with nonprofit organization staff and/or board members. Volunteering on advisory councils, boards, action committees, and faith-based groups focused on social justice can be an effective way to help you feel more culturally competent (Patel, 2007). All these opportunities give you the chance to learn about how various organizations approach social issues and what they are doing in terms of social action around these issues. You can learn if the approach they are employing is rooted in a particular ideology, philosophy, or paradigm; for example, a charity or social justice model (Marullo & Edwards, 2000), pedagogy of the oppressed (Freire, 1970), or social transformation (Williams, 2010). Reading through social media posts and feeds, newspapers, blogs, and other archived sources of community dialogue can help you navigate historical events and their relevance to various stakeholders in the community. Hanging out at various social gathering spots and engaging in casual conversations with longtime residents, as well as fellow newcomers, can be very enlightening.

As you begin to feel more competent in the culture of community and institution, you will be able to identify key areas where reciprocal partnerships can be enhanced or built around gaps in the community or institutional curricula and programs. You will be able to articulate opportunities that motivate both campus and community partners to invest in efforts to sustain mutually beneficial relationships. Eventually, reciprocal and sustainable partnerships can lead to more strategic and targeted efforts toward shared or collective impact around social issues in the community.

Community Partnerships

Multiple scholars from a range of academic disciplines have provided our field with a variety of lenses through which to view reciprocal partnerships and have suggested ways to build and sustain them (Bringle & Hatcher, 2002; Jacoby, 2003; Bushhouse, 2005). In the earlier years of the field, researchers identified important themes of mutuality and reciprocity, the social and economic benefits of community partnerships, and the motivations and benefits for both community partners and educational institutions through a longitudinal study examining community partnerships at 17 institutions (Gelmon, Holland, Seifer, Shinnamon, & Connors, 1998). Holland (2003) also provided the field with a helpful model that encouraged practitioners to ensure a feedback loop is created and maintained in partnerships.

More recently, scholars in the field have started to unpack what we mean by the concept of reciprocity, offering three areas of orientation within the concept of *exchange, influence, and generativity* (Dostilio et al., 2012). Reciprocal relationships, once a gold standard in partnerships, are now an expectation. We find that working toward "generativity-oriented reciprocity" by focusing on shared impact within a community is quickly becoming best practice in the field:

Exchange-oriented reciprocity: Participants give and receive something from the others that they would not otherwise have. In this orientation, reciprocity is the interchange of benefits, resources, or actions.

Influence-oriented reciprocity: The processes and/or outcomes of the collaboration are iteratively changed as a result of being influenced by the participants and their contributed ways of knowing and doing. In this orientation, reciprocity is expressed as a relational connection that is informed by personal, social, and environmental contexts.

Generativity-oriented reciprocity: As a function of the collaborative relationship, participants (who have or develop identities as co-creators) become and/or produce something new together that would not otherwise exist. This orientation may involve transformation of individual ways of knowing and being or the systems of which the relationship is a part. The collaboration may extend beyond the initial focus of outcomes as ways of knowing and systems of belonging evolve.

In generativity-oriented reciprocal partnerships, we see multifaceted campus-community connections that are more likely to be sustained and have greater impact on both organizations. Connections such as these are forged over time through creative endeavors, trust built over time, positive attitudes, and openness to new ideas by all parties involved (Bringle & Hatcher, 2002; Jacoby, 2003; Bushhouse, 2005).

These connections can be forged through outreach to community partners and internal (campus) stakeholders. When meeting with community partners, we have found a recommended approach is to listen closely and ask good questions. Often, when community partners first think about connecting with an institution, they think in terms of additional volunteers for positions already created within the organization. This is important; equally important is asking the community partner what—besides the already-established volunteering opportunities—might be venues for connections. What are the goals for the organization? What are back-burner projects the organization would like to work on/do, if only the time/resources/expertise existed? The answers to these questions begin to show the possibilities of what might be—and offer new avenues for student learning and development and community impact.

When establishing community partnerships, the empowerment of the community organization as an integral participant and co-educator is important for all stakeholders. Faculty members are focused on helping students meet the learning goals of their courses; the institution may have its own goals; and the community partner needs to meet its organizational priorities. The community innovator's job is to bring all stakeholders together in conversation; this provides a venue for idea generation and creative problem-solving and, perhaps most importantly, establishes a direct connection between the community organization and the institution, which increases the likelihood of the sustainability of the partnership and allows the community innovator to move to the background of this partnership and focus on other connections. A community innovator helps faculty see how campus-community partnerships can make deep learning happen because of its relevance to community implications, encourages institutional commitments to community goals, and ensures that community partners are deeply involved in the learning process.

External and Internal Promotion

What most people do not tell you when you begin this work is that a large percentage of their time is spent in sales. Now, do not get us wrong; it is not a door-to-door sales job selling overpriced vacuum cleaners. What we are selling is something we believe in—co-creating community innovations and partnerships that build on assets in the community and contribute to real change. But to be an effective community innovator and bring people together to work in culturally respectful, reciprocal partnerships, you have to be able to tell their story to both internal and external stakeholders, convincing them of the importance of the work and ensuring support. Stakeholder support can range from a president financially supporting a position and departmental budget, to a faculty member or community partner deciding to work with students on a sustainable partnership that goes beyond the typical volunteer placement at the organization.

There is much work involved in the promotion of campus-community partnerships on the grassroots, relationship-building level that can be effective. In addition, an excellent relationship with the marketing department on campus can help the community innovator with traditional marketing, social media, websites, news stories, and press releases.

The question, of course, becomes how to tell the story. Very helpful advice we have received is that cultural shifts at institutions of higher education are evolutions, not revolutions, so begin with what is already there: the mission statement. Mission statements are the driving force of the institution. All campus initiatives can be traced back to the mission statement, so it is essential to connect civic engagement work early—and often—to the mission of the institution.

A community innovator must also market his or her program to community partners and faculty, students, and staff at the institution. Marketing to campus—especially if a civic engagement, service-learning, or campus-community initiative is new or pervasively viewed in an old or inaccurate way—can be very challenging. What can work are person-to-person meetings and taking a lesson from grassroots organizing by joining everything. A diversity committee, the institutional effectiveness council, new-student orientation, faculty development workshop—these become venues for telling your story. While you must still protect your own time and efficiency, it is true that the more involved the community innovator is in a multitude of campus activities, the more ubiquitous the presence of your work and department. Remember faculty is not your only audience. Advisors and admissions counselors can help generate interest for students who want to get involved; student life staff could host a leadership series at which you could present; and maintenance employees will be essential for any large-scale event you host on campus.

Promoting your work to current and future community partners is also essential. The promotion of your work to community organizations involves educating community members about the mission of the institution and the nature of the reciprocal partnerships you desire to establish. This is especially important in contexts where a community partner might feel as if it must acquiesce to the demands of the institution; empowerment of community partners is key to the promotion of your program. Empowered (and satisfied) community partners will help spread the word to other community organizations.

In our opinion, there are a few essential elements to promotion that any community innovator must have:

- A dedicated webpage for civic engagement through the institution's website: At the beginning of a program's development, the institution's website may just be one page that describes the departmental mission and provides an overview of the program. Ideally, the website would evolve to include several webpages describing classes, projects, partners, and general information about the programs involving civic engagement at the college and would be regularly updated and maintained.

- A Facebook page: A similar progression could be established with social media. In the beginning, simply establishing a Facebook page might be the most that can be accomplished. As the program grows, the page may include descriptions of and pictures from the various partnerships that exist—a "database" for capturing the work that you're doing—and a way for you to connect to community partner organizations and talk about one anothers' projects and organizations, reaching an ever-greater audience.

- A blog: This can capture stories and add others' voices to the campus-community work a community innovator is doing. Stories of students, faculty, and community partners' experiences with partnerships are particularly beneficial.

- A good connection in the marketing department: Get to know someone on the marketing staff and set up regular meetings. Send meeting invitations to events; make sure that on- and off-campus campus-community partnership events are listed in the college calendar. Marketing colleagues will not come to everything, but they will come to some events and produce excellent pictures and a story write-up—maybe even on the institution's main landing page.

The goal for all of these grassroots, social media, and mainstream marketing techniques is to tell your story so you do not have to work so hard at telling your story alone. Others—faculty, students, staff, community partners—will start telling your story for you. That's when you know you have entered the cultural fibers of the institution and community.

Conclusion

We know the rapidly changing backdrop of higher education and the public's growing demand for accountability play a role in the evolution of expectations about the duties of a community innovator. We argue this shift in public perception of the sector is paving the way for civic engagement to take center stage. As summarized by Richard Guarasci, president of Wagner College, in his August 22, 2012, blog in the Huffington Post:

> Universities can help to demonstrate their relevance to an ever more skeptical public by ramping up civic engagement programs within their local communities and by creating specific partnerships. And, these partnerships are exactly what many communities need to help them grow and thrive amid tough economic times. This is a new moment in America: we have the opportunity to replace the usual town-gown tensions with a relationship that can benefit all (para. 2).

The field of civic engagement is ready for these changes; the theories and approaches are robust. There are already intersections between what we describe as a community innovator with social entrepreneurship and community development, and some imagine the possibility of these fields merging in the future. Civic engagement inquiry also intersects with fields of study examining social trends, working together to examine generative-oriented reciprocity. These connections, among others, empower the field of civic engagement to remain nimble and relevant. Indeed, during unprecedented times of uncertainty ahead for the higher education sector, community engagement professionals, in our role as community innovators, are uniquely positioned to assist our institutions navigating their roles in society.

Appendix 3A: Case Studies From the Field

Case Study 1: Widener University

Widener University, a 6,240-student private university located in Chester, Pennsylvania, provides an excellent example of an academic institution that has become an anchor institution in its community. Working with Chester, its members, and its leaders, Widener has forged reciprocal and sustained partnerships that are allowing the institution to work in and with the community to make collective impact.

Widener University and Chester did not always have a close relationship; indeed, at one time, Widener University had plans to build 8-foot, black iron fences around the campus, and the Chester community viewed Widener as an entity that "[ate] up land but [did]n't pay taxes" (Snyder, 2012, para. 12). However, when James T. Harris was named as the new president of the university, he committed that Widener would "be a better neighbor" and "striv[e] to build with its struggling host city" (Snyder, 2012, para. 13). The ways in which the city and university have partnered over the last decade have shown how Harris—and the faculty, staff, and students at Widener University—have made good on this promise.

Working from the inside out to promote engagement with the community, the Widener board of trustees established a civic engagement committee; faculty received money to redesign courses and connect curricula to local issues; and the recipients of Widener's highest scholarships went to students performing 300 hours of community service per year.

By 2012, more than 3,000 students had taken one or more of 70 courses tied to community-based projects. These community-based projects have included starting both a clinic and a K-7 charter school. The free clinic serves un- or under-insured people needing physical therapy; students in Widener's graduate program provide care under the direction of a licensed therapist. The charter school enrolls 350 students who continue to meet state standards for adequate yearly progress, with the help of nursing, clinical psychology, and social work students who assist there. Widener has also focused on education through the collaboration with other local colleges to start a college access center. Other collaborations with the city include the founding of a police substation in partnership with an area medical center and attracting a hotel and retail complex to the area.

This change did not come from Widener alone, but instead through partnership with the community. Widener has worked with state senators, mayors, school boards, and district leaders on the aforementioned projects, as well as state grant funders. A Widener instructor whose focus is social work and community organizing had her classes work at the grassroots level, "walk[ing] virtually every Chester block, surveying residents and assessing the location of key places such as food stores and youth programs" (Snyder, 2012, para. 18).

The effectiveness of Widener University's and Chester's partnership was recognized by Mark Linton, executive director of the White House Council on Strong Cities, which named Chester as one of six cities under President Obama's "Strong Cities, Strong Communities" plan aimed at spurring economic development. Linton recognized Widener as an *anchor institution*, *saying*, "Widener University was key in how we looked at the opportunities and what we can really do to help reinvent and build the economy" (Snyder, 2012, para. 9). Faculty on campus have noted there has been "tremendous change" in the relationship between Widener and its community—both are now willing to reach out to each other (Snyder, 2012, para. 9).

And that 8-foot, black iron fence? It never went up, and instead, an entrance to the campus was built facing a main thoroughfare, connecting the campus, both symbolically and physically, more closely to Chester.

Case Study 2: Inver Hills Community College and
Eagan and Lakeville Resource Center

The partnership between Inver Hills Community College in Inver Grove Heights, Minnesota, and one of the local food banks, the Eagan and Lakeville Resource Center, offers one example of a truly reciprocal partnership that has added capacity to both the academic institution and the nonprofit.

Inver Hills Community College (IHCC) serves a student body that is representative of the surrounding community: Its students are ethnically diverse; many are first-generation college students; and the majority of students are low-income. As determined by a food needs assessment survey done by the college in November 2012, 40% of students self-identified as needing food assistance, and an additional 17% said they did not need food but have in the past. Because hunger can affect school performance and retention, the college determined it was essential to meet this need.

Charged with meeting this campus need, IHCC's director of service-learning reached out to the Eagan and Lakeville Resource Center (ELRC), a local food bank and one of IHCC's longstanding community partners for the service-learning program. What has resulted is a multidimensional, multidisciplinary partnership between IHCC, ELRC, and the newly inaugurated IHCC/Metro State Interdisciplinary Community Garden, which is located on IHCC's campus.

The partnership is innovative in its simplicity: Each Wednesday, ELRC sends a mobile pantry stocked with food—70% of which is fresh—to campus, and this food is distributed to students who have self-identified as needing food support and completed an intake appointment through the counseling office. The beauty of this partnership is in the web of connections that have tied it together. ELRC grant applications are made stronger with IHCC's commitment of support. The community garden works with ELRC to provide individual plots for community members in need, as well as to determine what fresh produce would be most useful in summer and fall months and should be planted in the community space. IHCC and Metropolitan State University service-learning students taking classes in psychology, communication, human services, biology, and education work in the community garden and at ELRC as food shoppers and benefits screeners. Entire classes of students at IHCC throw, fire, and glaze bowls for ELRC's "Empty Bowls" fundraising event (ceramics); collect data to provide a comprehensive view of impoverishment in Dakota County (statistics); do soil testing, grow seedlings, and research composting techniques (environmental biology); and give short, informative speeches about the mobile pantry at IHCC (public speaking). IHCC leverages student work-study hours to support the community garden and on site at ELRC, each receiving a minimum of 20 hours of student support each week. In addition, student groups on campus work closely with ELRC to promote the mobile pantry and energize campus in an institution-wide food drive.

The partnership can also be seen at the advisory level. The IHCC Foundation and ELRC have long shared a board member who has connections to both communities, but now, the connections have grown significantly. ELRC has a seat at the table of the Service-Learning Advisory Board at IHCC, and the vice president of student affairs at IHCC now serves on the ELRC board.

This partnership was established by looking at the community through an assets-based model for community development. It exemplifies a sustainable, mutually beneficial model that meets a community need and increases college access and success, while promoting community development. This is a long-term campus-community partnership for the common good that involves a comprehensive and innovative way to bring campus and community together through community-based learning and meeting community needs—even on IHCC's own campus. Low-income IHCC students benefit from food resources and the training counselors received from ELRC on available community resources. Moreover, all IHCC students can benefit from experiential learning opportunities offered through the service-learning, volunteer, and work-study programs that connect IHCC to ELRC and the community garden.

Appendix 3B: Reflection Questions

Novice Professionals:

- Where is my institution in the process of institutionalizing civic engagement, and how do campus-community partnerships fit into this bigger picture?

- How do campus-community partnerships fit into the fabric of my institution? How will/do they support/operationalize its mission?

- Where are the greatest strengths and challenges at my institution in relation to building and sustaining campus-community partnerships?

- What are the community's goals for partnering with my work? What do I think they really want?

- How do I think the multiple sub-communities I work on view my institution? How do they perceive my campus's interests/goals?

- Why is the marketing/storytelling of civic engagement on campus important to my department/the college? What are my goals when telling the civic engagement story?

- Who are my target audiences for telling the story of civic engagement work? Who are the audiences off campus? On campus?

- Where are my gaps in knowledge/skills, and where are my strengths as a professional in the field of community organizing? How can I improve my gaps in knowledge? Capitalize on my strengths?

Intermediate Professionals:

- With whom could I develop a sustained relationship—one that lasts several semesters/years? How can I start that conversation?

- How does my institution approach partnerships? In what ways do I want to see my institution transformed by partnerships?

- Who could be reciprocal partners in the process of filling persisting weaknesses and gaps in best practice at my institution?

- How could involvement with specific social issues support and enhance campus curriculum, programs, and the direction in which my institution wants to go in the future?

- What do I believe determines the quality of a community partnership? How is my institution assessing the quality of community partnerships and civic engagement experiences?

- Who is responsible for telling the story of civic engagement on campus? From whom is the story most effective?

- Who are my allies at my institution (maintenance, student life, marketing, etc.)? How can civic engagement programs capitalize on these internal partnerships?

Advanced Professionals:

- How can social issues ripe for collective impact efforts in my community inform my institution's curriculum and program planning for the future?

- How do I include community partners as co-educators? Are community partners empowered as co-educators by my institution? What could I do on campus to reinforce to students the importance of community partners as co-educators?

- What do I see as the role of an anchor institution in the community? What do I see as my institution's role in my community?

- How can best practice in cultural competencies, community partnerships, and internal and external promotion be shared to help influence the field of civic engagement to broaden its current scope?

About the Authors

Maggie Baker has served as service learning coordinator at Loras College since August 2006. She has developed the institutional and community infrastructure necessary to support academically embedded community-based learning and reciprocal, strategic partnerships. Prior to coming to Loras, Maggie was the first director of community service and internships at Buena Vista University. She received her B.S. in family and consumer sciences from the University of Arizona and her M.A. in social sciences from the Universiteit van Amsterdam in the Netherlands.

Katie Halcrow has served as the director of service learning at Inver Hills Community College since 2012. She received her B.A. in mathematics from Wake Forest University, her M.A. in German languages and literatures from The Ohio State University, and her M.F.A. in creative writing from Hamline University. She loves her job as director of service-learning and the opportunity it affords her to hone her creative tendencies to craft projects that allow students to provide meaningful, relevant service to a community partner, while putting the knowledge and skills they are attaining in their coursework into practice.

References

Battistoni, R. M. (2002). *Civic engagement across the curriculum: A resource book for service learning faculty in all disciplines.* Providence, RI: Campus Compact, Brown University.

Boyer, E. L. (1990). *Scholarship reconsidered: Priorities of the professoriate.* Princeton, NJ: Carnegie Foundation for the Advancement of Teaching.

Bringle, R. G., & Hatcher, J. A. (2002). Campus-community partnerships: The terms of engagement. *Journal of Social Issues, 58,* 503-516.

Bushouse, B. K. (2005). *Community nonprofit organizations and service-learning: resource constraints to building partnerships with universities.* Ann Arbor, MI: Scholarly Publishing Office, University of Michigan Library.

Dewey, J. (1916). *Democracy and education.* New York, NY: The Free Press.

Dostilio, L. D., Brackmann, S. M., Edwards, K. E., Harrison, B., Kliewer, B. W., & Clayton, P. H. (2012). *Saying what we mean and meaning what we say.* Retrieved from http://quod.lib.umich.edu/m/mjcsl/3239521.0019.102/11/--reciprocity-saying-what-we-mean-and-meaning what-we-say?page=root;size=100;view=text

Enos, S., & Morton, K. (2003). Developing a theory and practice of campus-community partnerships. In B. Jacoby & Associates (Eds.), *Building partnerships for service learning* (20-41). San Francisco, CA: John Wiley & Sons, Inc.

Freire, P. (1970). *Pedagogy of the oppressed.* New York, NY: Herder and Herder.

Gelmon, S. B., Holland, B. A., Seifer, S. D., Shinnammon, A. F., & Connors, K. (1998, Fall). Community-university partnerships for mutual learning. *Michigan Journal of Community Service Learning, 5,* 97-107

Guarasci, R. (2012). How can colleges spark economic and community development? *Huffington Post.* Retrieved from http://www.huffingtonpost.com/richard-guarasci/college-community-engagement-_b_1821358.html

Jacoby, B. (2003). *Building partnerships for service-learning.* San Francisco, CA: Jossey-Bass.

Kania, J., & Kramer, M. (2011). *Collective impact | Stanford social innovation review.* Retrieved from http://www.ssireview.org/articles/entry/collective_impact

Langseth, M. & Plater, W.M. (2004). *Public work and the academy: An academic administrator's guide to civic engagement and service-learning.* San Francisco, CA: Jossey-Bass.

Marullo, S., & Edwards, B. (2000). From charity to justice. *American Behavioral Scientist, 43*(5), 89.

Maurrasse, D. (2007). *Leveraging anchor institutions for urban success.* Chicago, IL: CEOs for Cities. Retrieved from http://community-wealth.org/content/city-anchors-leveraging-anchor-institutions-urban-success

Maurrasse, D. J. (2001). *Beyond the campus: How colleges and universities form partnerships with their communities.* New York, NY: Routledge.

The National Task Force on Civic Learning and Democratic Engagement (2012). *A crucible moment: College learning and democracy's future.* Washington, DC: Association of American Colleges and Universities. Retrieved from *http://www.aacu.org/civic_learning/crucible/*

Patel, E. (2007). *Acts of faith.* Boston, MA: Beacon Press.

Snyder, S. (2012, December 5). *Widener, Chester forging close community ties. The Philadelphia Inquirer.* Retrieved from http://articles.philly.com/2012-12-05/news/35597211_1_widener-student-james-t-harris-iii-widener-university

Stoecker, R., & Tryon, E. (2009). The unheard voices: Community organizations and service learning. Philadelphia, PA: Temple University Press

Tryon, E., & Stoecker, R. (2007). Community standards for service learning. Retrieved from comm-org.wisc.edu/sl/files/cs4slbrochure.pdf

Williams, A. K. (2010). *Framing deep change: Essays on transformative social change.* Berkeley, CA: The Center for Transformative Change.

Worrall, L. (2007). *Asking the community: A case study of community partner perspectives.* Retrieved from http://quod.lib.umich.edu/m/mjcsl/3239521.0014.101?rgn=main;view=fulltext

Critical Response: Community Innovator

Randy Stoecker, Ph.D., Professor, Department of Community and Environmental Sociology, University of Wisconsin

For the past three decades, I've been attempting to collaborate with various kinds of groups and organizations around a myriad of issues. And for the past two, I've been actively working with faculty, administrators, and students, attempting to do similar work through a wide variety of higher education institutions in a wide variety of places. I reflect on my and others' work continuously, and I have never been able to shake a sense of discomfort with our approaches and our outcomes. My sense of discomfort, in this case, extends to the term "community innovator." The term feels too individualistic, too lacking in collaboration, too one-directional. And I know that's not what these authors mean. But the term is useful in helping me confront a deeper discomfort—one that is not simply about words, but about my identity and my work and, perhaps, the work of others as well.

Where does my discomfort start? It starts with my realization I am not a member of any of the "communities" that I work with. I am a white male with a tenured faculty position at a highly ranked university. I live in a "nice" neighborhood. And this is true, in varying degrees, for most of us in academia, except for those rare individuals who have grown up where they are working, without the race, sex, class, ability, and other privileges characteristic of most academics, and still live among those they grew up with. So, I have come to learn that the first thing I need to do when I engage with a group of people through my professional role is to facilitate their innovation, not mine. The first thing every struggling group needs is to take control over the process of improving their condition because the fundamental cause of their current condition is their lack of power. Power rests in controlling the agenda, and controlling the agenda depends on being able to define the problem, define the solution, lead the implementation of the solution, and lead the evaluation of the solution. As the privileged higher ed "partner," I don't have to live with the direct consequences of the solution. So, if my work is not supporting the expansion of the group's power, then I am part of the problem, not part of the solution.

So, the best I can say is that I consider myself an "innovator's helper." On my more pessimistic days, I analogize that to the "plumber's helper." On my more optimistic ones, I get to feel like the person who brings the tools and supplies (and sometimes new techniques) to the carpenter, which, to me is a grassroots group working for a more just society. I'm not building the building—the on-the-ground social justice work. I'm bringing the support that makes it easier to build the building. In my case, that normally means I bring research. And I mean research in the broadest possible way—something I've taken to calling knowledge mobilization (following my Canadian and European friends) because the process is less about following the rules of academic research, and more about gathering information and facilitating a group to take that information and turn it into knowledge they can use to pursue their goals.

Consequently, I also feel uncomfortable with the terms "partnership" and "reciprocity," at least in the way they are used in this context. For me, the terms imply an assumption of equality, and I just can't wrap my head around what is equal about a "partnership" between an un- or under-funded grassroots group and, in my case, a multi-billion-dollar higher education institution. Such power dimensions remain even with small higher education institution in rural areas that are often one of the largest employers, largest landowners, and can exert far more than their share of influence over local commerce, Worse, we have come to use "reciprocity" to describe a relationship where higher education and community groups come together for an exchange—they partner for separate goals and take away different products from the relationship—usually some kind of volunteer hours and a report on the community side and student learning on the higher education side. That is distinctly different from a collaboration where all parties are working for the same goal—especially when that goal is social justice.

Finally, as I continue to do this work, I also feel increasingly funny even using the word "community." As this chapter reflects, we have continued to complicate our ideas of "community," and I'm not sure we have anything approaching what should be the standard for "community" any more. So, instead of working "with communities," I think of *working with constituencies toward community*. And, if I am successful, then someday, we will be writing about constituencies that used to be oppressed, exploited, and excluded as true communities and their members as community innovators. Those of us engaged with such people can then feel proud to have contributed, from the background, because those community voices are now being heard as easily as the voices from corporations, governments, and even higher education institutions that used to drown them out.

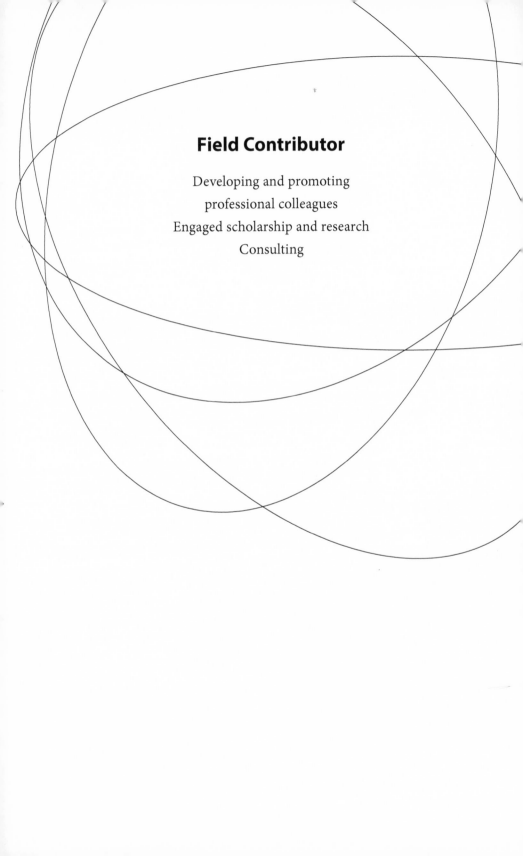

Field Contributor

Developing and promoting
professional colleagues
Engaged scholarship and research
Consulting

Chapter 4: Field Contributor

Kate DeGraaf and Laurel Hirt

As we can all attest to, over the last 20 years, the field of civic engagement and service-learning has evolved and will continue to change. It is evident through the development of programs and collaborations on publications such as *A Crucible Moment: College Learning and Democracy's Future* (National Task Force on Civic Learning and Democratic Engagement, 2012). The development is not only due to the fact that more research is being produced, but it is also the changing environments and communities in which we live (Cowens, 2013). As the field develops and changes throughout the next few generations, we see great opportunities for creativity and innovation. We define a field contributor as someone who is able to provide encouragement, mentorship, research, data, consulting, or other aspects that contribute to increasing positive change in the field of civic engagement. Each individual brings a unique perspective and set of abilities that can assist in the development of the field, and we need to be sure to share that valuable information and insight. Whether you work at a research institution, a community college, or supporting organization such as Campus Compact, there is something that can be contributed to support our changing field.

Each day a professional in the field has to be an organizational manager, institutional strategic leader, and community innovator, which can leave little time to contribute to the greater field. Time can be a challenge, but if we can each set a little aside to give back to our field, we will be able to have lasting impact as community engagement professionals.

For the field of civic engagement to have sustained development, each individual has an opportunity and responsibility to contribute. We find role models across the country who are well-known researchers and writers or the people we look forward to seeing present at conferences. There are many ways and paths you can follow or create as a field contributor. To help our profession grow, we need to expand our ideas and acknowledge the countless ways we can give back to the field. The following skill sets listed below should be nurtured:

Developing and promoting professional colleagues

Engaged scholarship and research

Consulting

Developing and Promoting Professional Colleagues

Professional development has become a buzzword in many fields, but it is integral to individuals within any career or field. To sustain the field of civic engagement, we need not only to be growing as professionals, but also be striving to mentor and cultivate others to bring in new perspectives and creativity to challenge us all as we do our collective work. This can be achieved in a variety of ways. Some of the skills that assist in developing professionals in the field are facilitation of leadership development in others, guiding reflection, relationship-building, and communication.

From the start of your career, there are ways to connect with other professionals through respective state or regional Campus Compact meetings, regional or national conferences, or by reaching out to other civic engagement offices or professionals. Engage with communities of practice that allow you to carve out the time and space for reflection on your own practice. By making these connections, you can gain mentors and become a mentor for others. Networks and learning communities can create a valuable and much-needed support system in this line of work, especially for individuals who find themselves in one-person offices or isolated without other colleagues in the nearby region.

As you grow as a professional, you will be able to be a role model to students taking courses or participating in civic engagement programs, to mentor student workers, AmeriCorps members, or colleagues at different institutions. You will be able to seek out advice and share your own experiences concerning what paths other professionals took to get to where they are today. Connections might help you decide if an investment in further education is a worthwhile choice to make or if a program you are running can be a model for the field. As your experience grows, there will be opportunities for you to develop programs that build capacity in our field. The Campus Compact publication *Students as Colleagues* (2006) provides many great examples of ways institutions have developed programs that give students valuable learning and leadership experiences in community and civic engagement offices. These opportunities foster the growth of potential future professionals.

Engaged Scholarship and Research

The production of engaged scholarship to advance the field of community and civic engagement has expanded over the years. In the late 1990s, a small number of scholars in community engagement were beginning to publish important scholarship for the field (e.g., Holland, Bringle, Eyler, Giles, Sandmann, and Harkavy). Organizations such as the International Association for Research on Service-Learning and Community Engagement (IARSLCE) and organizations with a narrower scope such as Imaging America have been launched to bring engaged and public scholars together to share their work with one another and to blaze a trail for emerging scholars through efforts to promote promising graduate students. Through the work of these associations and others, the field has significantly expanded in number and breadth of contributions to "community-engaged scholarship" and the "scholarship of engagement."

While these two terms are often used interchangeably due in part to Ernest Boyer's 1996 article "The Scholarship of Engagement" in the *Journal of Public Service and Outreach's* first issue, over the years, the terms have come to be understood in a more nuanced manner. Community-engaged scholarship most often results from community-engaged scholarly activities (such as community-based participatory action research) that can be communicated in discipline-specific journals and outlets. The results can also reach members of the community through policy briefs and educational campaigns that allow the research to be more accessible to the audiences that might benefit most from the research itself.

In the scholarship of engagement, practitioner-scholars publish research related to the field of civic and community engagement and the process of supporting engaged teaching and learning. An example of this could include writing an article about establishing and sustaining partnerships between your institution and a particular neighborhood that required a significant amount of relationship and trust-building before any activity occurred between your institution and the neighborhood. The Campus Compact 2001 publication by Kerrissa Heffernan titled *Fundamentals of Service-Learning Course Construction* could be considered to be a product-based guide resulting from the scholarship of engagement.

While the *Michigan Journal on Community Service-Learning*, published by the University of Michigan since 1994, represents the first peer-reviewed journal in the field, many others, both online and in print form, have come into being over the years to provide a range of opportunities for scholars to pursue as publication outlets. It is important that we use the data we collect through evaluation and assessment by analyzing them and sharing the results. Acknowledging our contributions of data and research can help us tell the story of what we are doing and the impact we are having on college campuses and in our communities. Journals and conference presentations are two ways the data and findings can be disseminated. As a newer professional, it is important to spend time reading research and engaged scholarship so you will be able to contribute and build upon the work already developed. Spending time reviewing the research will also assist in the learning process and should help you identify pertinent questions, hypotheses, and gaps in the field that can lead to further engaged research opportunities to advance the field.

Documenting our successful and unsuccessful practices within community and civic engagement in higher education can be very illustrative for other practitioners. Being honest about our failures and mistakes when doing engaged work can be challenging, but we can all do better, more thoughtful work with communities when we share our shortcomings and document our successes more readily. This allows us to take advantage of prior lessons learned and benefit from them as we move forward in our work.

For a more extensive discussion about the role of research in building the civic and community engagement field, see Billig, Moely, and Holland's (2009) chapter on "Research Informing Practice" in *Creating Our Identities in Service-Learning and Community Engagement.* This chapter also identifies the importance of establishing associations such as the International Association for Research on Service-Learning and Civic Engagement as a place for researchers to come together and share their work to deepen and expand their scholarship. For other, more in-depth explanations of the scholarship of engagement and criteria for engaged scholarship, see Crews (2011) "Reflections on Scholarship and Engaged Scholarship: A Call to the Field," where he expands on Boyer's earlier work and articulates that this form of scholarship "both involves and benefits the community; it is scholarship that is in service to the community...not just on the community" as has been seen most frequently in other research (p. 330). Having a more thorough understanding of the research informing our field's growth and the frameworks that led to the articulation of the scholarship of engagement and engaged scholarship are necessary for successful field contribution.

Consulting

Acting as a consultant to another institution or organization is a common way to contribute to the growth of our field. Practitioners with years of experience at one institution or several can provide valuable insight to institutions looking to expand their current efforts. Consulting can be for a specific program or course, but it can also assist with the development of an office or be part of larger, ongoing efforts designed to help with institutionalization of community engagement efforts on campuses.

While we often think of consultants in a formal sense, this work often begins informally on a program level through individual connections at conferences, email exchanges, or phone calls to other practitioners to find out how people run particular aspects of their programs. These informal networking connections can be a way for a newer practitioner to start establishing groundwork for the future while gaining diversity of thought and new ideas to improve his or her work. Consultants can be used in more formal ways to develop and run faculty development programs, assist with strategic planning efforts of offices and centers, or to facilitate an external review of your institution's community engagement program.

As we consult with different schools and programs, it is important to remember that each institution and the communities within which it is situated have unique cultures. A consultant needs to have expertise and a passion for the work. Strong listening skills, the ability to ask good and challenging questions, and experience in facilitating discussions are needed to assist others when participating in the consulting process. Focus groups, evaluations, and interviews can be used to assist in the process. Consultants also need to have strong communication skills, problem-solving skills, the ability to market oneself, excellent interpersonal skills, observation skills, a proven ability to be objective, and the organization and time management skills needed to assist in providing valuable feedback to the contracting entity.

Advice for How to Be a Field Contributor

Get in front of people and let them see your passion for your work. The more people who see you talking about your work and believe you are doing good work, the more visible you will become as a potential consultant. When people are looking to hire a consultant or asking around about potential consultants to other colleagues, it will help to be a person others know and remember. As a new professional, it is important to connect with other colleagues and hear about what is being done in the field to know where the gaps exist. Build your network by getting to know a lot of people who are doing interesting work and explore possibilities to collaborate, co-facilitate a workshop, or present at a conference session together. This can be especially useful for newer professionals. You can put yourself in front of others in the field by presenting skills-based workshops at pre-conference sessions for professional organization conferences such as the American College Personnel Association, National Association for Student Personnel Administrators, Community-Campus Partnerships for Health, and at Campus Compact regional meetings or leading and facilitating webinars.

Make it known you are interested in taking on opportunities outside your position. If you want to be more involved in the field, let your mentors or other key people at state or regional Campus Compact offices know. Volunteer on committees inside and outside of higher education. If your state or region has many civic engagement efforts occurring in K-12 education or in the larger community, these are places to explore what is happening in the broad civic engagement field.

One of the most important ways to learn and challenge our field to grow is by being involved in other sectors and looking for opportunities where synergies can emerge. As you volunteer to take on new opportunities, you will become known for your actions and will be recommended for future possibilities.

Be willing to take risks and share both successes and failures with others in the work so we can all benefit and learn from one another. Trista Harris, executive director of the Minnesota Council on Foundations, was one of the keynotes at the 20th Anniversary Celebration and Summit of Minnesota Campus Compact. In her speech, which was titled "A Leader's Guide to Shaping the Future," she echoed both of our featured champions by encouraging us to get outside of our higher education bubble and use knowledge from other fields. We have to be open to innovation and sharing successes and challenges openly. She encouraged the audience not to be afraid to fail. As Julie Plaut, executive director of Minnesota Campus Compact, regularly shares through events and informal conversations, practitioners need to make their voices heard and, therefore, must model critical reflection. One of the best ways to do that in higher education is to publish. Online tools can help you share your practice and encourage more people to take advantage of what has already been created. Models can be replicated or tweaked to apply to one's respective audience.

Commit to setting time aside to be a contributor to the field. Practitioners are busy people, and rarely do they go more than a day without trying to accomplish more than is possible. If you are new to the field, start by educating yourself by reading articles and books, talking to other practitioners on campuses in your area or at other peer (or aspirational peer) institutions, and attending workshops and conferences. Start small and keep expanding. As you educate yourself and learn more by running your own programs and seeing what others do, you can apply to present on your programs and write about what you are doing and your process so others can learn from your efforts. Carving out time to do these things does not happen unless you make it a priority for yourself and your unit. If raising your personal visibility and that of your colleagues and your center is a goal, set up a plan for yourself and your unit for where you want to be in three to five years. It will be beneficial to come up with a set of timelines and concrete outcomes that will allow you (and your collaborators) to articulate the best ways to leverage new and already-existing data, research, and writing. Make sure you look ahead to when deadlines for abstracts and proposals are due and commit to a concrete plan.

Appendix 4A: Case Studies From the Field

Author's note: In deciding who to feature as examples of field contributors, we reflected on our network of colleagues from across the country and decided to highlight two women who have taken different career paths, but both emphasized the importance of sharing one's "voice" with the field and the crucial place relationship-building and making spaces for conversations among peers have in being strong field contributors. The following case studies are the result of two interviews with the colleagues.

Case Study 1: Julie Plaut - Claim the Power of Your Voice and Encourage Avenues to Contribute Your Experiences

As an experienced professional in community and civic engagement, I have worked as an undergraduate student leader/instructor of service-learning, as a graduate student leader in a start-up office on a campus, in a state Compact office, for the national Campus Compact, and as a consultant to other Compacts and institutions of higher education for close to 25 years. I regularly encourage practitioners to claim their own experientially informed voices. I have often found community engagement professionals are reluctant to write and to publish, and I admit to being nervous about writing myself because of academia's expert culture. Yet, I firmly believe that if we really want to be a field that respects and builds on diverse sources of knowledge and advances collaborative change, we need to be willing to admit mistakes and document our learnings by writing, sharing resources with others, and learning from other disciplines and fields. In my work at Minnesota Campus Compact, I regularly promote opportunities for practitioners to contribute to the field by hosting publishing workshops, inviting people personally to contribute to specific publications, helping them to find sources that make sense for their topics, and working with them to guide them through the process. I encourage practitioners to reflect on their experiences, insights, and existing sources of data, as well as to identify the gaps in the literature as a valuable approach when considering how a practitioner can make a unique contribution to the field. With the growth of online technologies, blogs, forums, webinars, and open educational resources such as Minnesota Campus Compact's Civic Leadership Initiative Online (CLIO) website can make the idea of publishing less overwhelming and much more accessible to larger audiences.

Through Minnesota Campus Compact, I have created opportunities for practitioners to come together in peer coaching circles, as well as a yearlong learning community, to support one another's professional development. I also invite other nonprofit and community leaders to share their perspectives and leverage partnerships with other institutions to make it possible for units to participate in opportunities locally that would often be cost-prohibitive to attend. Additionally I invite "boundary-spanners" into discussion with people in the field to foster new thinking and innovation.

Case Study 2: Megan Voorhees - Enthusiastically Share Resources, Actively Contribute Your Knowledge of the Field With Colleagues, and Mentor Student Leaders by Encouraging Their Voices

When I first started in my role as the director of a small center that was primed to grow, we believed sharing our resources with others was one of the best ways we could contribute our expertise to the larger field. One of the first things the Cal Corps Public Service Center did was put together an online student leadership toolkit and told people it was there to use and adapt to their institutional environment. I told people to try out our resources and share with us how they adapted them, and we would update the information each year so everyone could benefit. I still believe this approach is one of the most useful practices to implement for people in the field. The year before I left my position with the Cal Corps Public Service Center, the center worked with several consultants to create a faculty handbook to assist faculty and centers in designing community-engaged courses. The resource was sent to colleagues across the country, and practitioners were asked to share how they've used it or adapted it, with the intent to update it online, as we had done with the earlier student leadership toolkit.

My work to champion the role of student leadership and voice in public service did not happen by accident. Having been a student leader at Lewis & Clark College, where I founded and ran the student-run Volunteer Service Center in the early 1990s, I know the value students bring to their campuses and their community projects. Mentoring student leaders is one of the things I found great satisfaction in doing. I think traditional-aged college students are often in a great place in their lives to take on leadership roles in community engagement, if we make opportunities available for them to do so on our campuses. When I left UC Berkeley, my center had more than 175 student staff running programs.

Sharing experience and knowledge with others through many different forums has been a hallmark of my work as a practitioner. I have done this through presenting at conferences, facilitating retreats for other professionals in the field, benchmarking the Public Service Center among its peer institutions, facilitating strategic planning processes, participating in external reviews, and by serving on search committees at other institutions. As a practitioner, one of the most valuable things I think we can do for the future of our field is to create more spaces for people to come together and build relationships with one another through deeper conversations. It may sound like a luxury to say this, but it's essential. We need to be able to find places to rejuvenate and re-energize so we can continue to do quality work in the world.

Appendix 4B: Reflection Questions

Novice Professionals

- What associations or conferences do I want to connect with to assist my growth as a professional in the field?

- What are ways I can rearrange my time to create space to learn best practices and contribute to the field?

- What can I do to prepare myself to publish on the scholarship of engagement? To begin to think about salient community-engaged research topics?

- Who could be a mentor or role model I could learn from in the field? Who can I mentor?

- What courses should I take to prepare me to give back to the field? How will I stay up-to-date on the latest research?

Intermediate Professionals

- Are there any associations, conference committees, or grant review committees locally or state-wide I should join?

- What are ways I can share best practices with others across my state?

- What current work or data am I collecting that can contribute to the field? Have I learned any hard lessons from mistakes I have made that others can learn from? How should I go about sharing this information in the most useful way possible?

- Who can I mentor in the field? Do I have a student who stands out? Is there a new professional at another school?

- What leadership roles am I taking in my institution or state Compact?

Advanced Professionals

- Are there any associations, conference committees, or grant reviews nationally I should join?

- What best practices can I share nationally through a publication?

- What work am I doing or what research can I produce in my community or state to promote civic engagement?

- Are there classes I could create at the undergraduate level or graduate level to provide leadership development for future professionals?

- Is there a program or conference I can create and develop for professionals in the field? Are people in my area eager to participate in a multi-day retreat or a yearlong learning community I could launch and co-facilitate with other colleagues?

About the Authors

Kate DeGraaf serves as the service-learning manager at Kellogg Community College. Kate received her undergraduate degree from Cornerstone University, where she majored in language arts and obtained her elementary education teaching certificate. After teaching fourth grade, she received her master's degree in college student affairs leadership from Grand Valley State University. Through her work at Kellogg Community College, she has been able to assist with institutionalizing service-learning. Kate is on various community boards and the Michigan Campus Compact Network Committee. Kate enjoys baking, training for triathlons, traveling, exploring the outdoors, and learning about new cultures.

Laurel Hirt is the director of the Community Service-Learning Center at the University of Minnesota-Twin Cities. Laurel represented the University of Minnesota-Twin Cities in the work to pilot the Community Engagement Classification System led by the Carnegie Foundation for the Advancement of Teaching. She serves on the board of the Higher Education Consortium for Urban Affairs (HECUA) and is the governing council chair for Pierre Bottineau French Immersion School, the first self-governed school in Minnesota. Laurel received Minnesota Campus Compact's 2005 Sister Pat Kowalski Leadership Award for Advancing Service-Learning and Community-Campus Partnerships and the President's Award for Outstanding Service to the University of Minnesota in 2008.

References

Billig, S. H., Moely, B .E., & Holland, B. A. (2009). Research informing practice: Developing practice standards and guidelines for improving service-learning and community engagement. In S. H. Billig, B. E. Moely, & B. A. Holland (Eds.), *Creating our identities in service-learning and community engagement.* (265-282). Charlotte, NC: Information Age Publishing.

Boyer, E. (1996). The scholarship of engagement. *Journal of Public Service and Outreach, 1*(1), 11-20.

Cowens, S. S. (2013). Reimagining Tulane as an engaged community partner. *AAC&U Diversity and Democracy, 16*(1).
Retrieved from http://www.aacu.org/diversitydemocracyvol16no1/cowen.cfm

Crew, R. J. (2011). Reflections on scholarship and engaged scholarship: A call to the field. In T. Stewart & N. Webster (Eds.), *Problematizing service-learning: Critical reflections for development and action* (325-342). Charlotte, NC: Information Age Publishing.

Heffernan, K. (2001). *Fundamentals of service-learning course construction.* Providence, RI: Campus Compact, Brown University.

The National Task Force on Civic Learning and Democratic Engagement. (2012). A crucible moment: College learning and democracy's future. Washington, DC: Association of American Colleges and Universities. Retrieved from http://www.aacu.org/civic_learning/crucible/

Zlotkowski, E., Longo, N., & Williams, J. R. (Eds.). (2006). *Students as colleagues: Expanding the circle of service-learning leadership.* Providence, RI: Campus Compact, Brown University.

Critical Response: Field Contributor

Julie Hatcher, Ph.D., Executive Director, Center for Service and Learning, Indiana University-Purdue University Indianapolis

In the past 20 years, the work associated with service-learning has grown into a much broader field, now encompassing community engagement, public scholarship, and the role of anchor institutions in civil society. During this time, I have had the good fortune of being engaged in a very meaningful career. Many of us have worked together as field builders, and it is quite rewarding to see how, in fact, the field has grown over time, with deeper roots and more fruitful expressions.

An early mantra among colleagues in the field of service-learning was "We find our way by walking." Collectively, we had a sense that we were navigating unchartered territory and that we needed to depend on one another to learn how the work should be done. We freely shared advice, program strategies, and resources. This collective action built a vibrant association of professionals like you who are dedicated to advancing the public purposes of higher education.

In terms of being a field builder, however, my experience is that "We find our way by writing." As a professional staff member in the Office of Service Learning in 1993, one of the early steps in our campus action plan was to offer faculty development workshops. I called national Campus Compact to request materials, only to learn that, at that point in time, there were no faculty development materials available. When I shared this with Bob Bringle, our faculty director, his immediate response was "Great. There is a gap in the field, and we can contribute to filling it." So, for the next few weeks, I gathered and read resources on reflection (e.g., Brookfield, Dewey, Kolb, Schon) and created a presentation to share with others.

Immediately following the workshop, which had attracted about a dozen participants, Bob said quite clearly, "Nice workshop, Julie, but now you need to write an article so others can learn from your work." That challenge and expectation, along with his guidance and mentoring, created a disposition and practice within our work that continues today. Needless to say, it was a laborious process to write my first article, but I found it to be a rewarding process to create a finished product. I discovered it is the process, not the end product, that is most meaningful to my professional development.

In 1999, I served as co-editor for a curriculum guide published by Indiana Campus Compact. Similar to this volume, the curriculum guide was developed in collaboration with others and included presentation materials to use in faculty development workshops. In 2002, we had the opportunity to be a part of the Community Higher Education Service Program in South Africa. This international faculty development program partnered U.S. and South African universities to integrate service into the curriculum. When Bob and I arrived in Bloemfontein, South Africa, our host greeted us with joy. He had just received copies of the curriculum guide for each participant, and as he held them up, he said, "This is like gold." That, perhaps, was the first time I understood the true value of scholarship. Our ideas had the ability to travel around the world because they were in print.

Knowledge is a funny thing. Knowledge grows when you give it away. It becomes more complex and deepens overtime, and it comes to life when it is put into print through PowerPoints, brochures, blog posts, or articles. Knowledge is a powerful resource that, when used correctly, opens doors, builds others' capacity, and improves and refines our practice. Knowledge has a public purpose.

As civic-minded professionals, I believe we have a responsibility to be a "social trustee of knowledge" if we want to collectively build and sustain the field of community engagement. If you are reading this essay, I am quite confident you are a civic-minded professional. And you likely share generously with others, in informal ways, what you have learned through practice. This chapter will challenge you to ramp it up a notch and devote time, energy, and creativity to sharing your knowledge in formal ways.

There are many good ideas in this chapter, yet there are a couple of additional points I would like to share. The first is to reinforce that you need not approach this work on your own. Like all engagement, I think scholarship is best done with others. Others can test our thoughts, debate the details, question our approach, hold us accountable to timelines, create ideas, and wordsmith definitions. And secondly, scholarship takes the investment of time…extra time beyond your current job description. It typically requires nights, weekends, or devoted periods to push through the completion of an article, chapter, or presentation. However, it is precisely that push that helps me to clarify my ideas and reconfirms my own dedication to the work.

As a field builder, act upon your curiosities, invest the time, work with others, and discover the joy of sharing your knowledge.

Professional Development Resources

Chapter 5: Professional Development Resources

In creating this resource, we realize it will be neither the beginning nor the end of any professional's development and self-reflection journey. To that end, our team of professionals pulled together their best ideas for ongoing professional development. For further reading, please see the reference sections throughout the book, where authors have cited sources that guided their chapters and their professional lives. Below you will find additional ideas for resources you can find online, conferences you can attend, publication opportunities, and other, more experiential ideas, that are "beyond the typical."

Online Resources

- *AAC&U Civic Institutional Matrix*
  www.aacu.org/civic_learning/crucible/documents/civicmatrix.pdf

- *AAC&U Values Rubric*
  www.aacu.org/value/rubrics/pdf/All_Rubrics.pdf

- *Advanced Service-Learning Toolkit for Academic Leaders*
  Barbara Holland (2001): compact.org/advancedtoolkit/default.html

- *American Association for Community Colleges, Creating a Climate for Service Learning Success*
  www.aacc.nche.edu/Resources/aaccprograms/horizons/Documents/creatingaclimate_082010.pdf

- *Asset-Based Community Development Institute School of Education and Social Policy, Northwestern University*
  www.abcdinstitute.org

- *Bonner Foundation*
  www.bonner.org

- *Break Away*
  www.alternativebreaks.org

- *Building Effective Community Campus Partnerships*
  depts.washington.edu/ccph/pdf_files/Nebraska%20Building%20Effective%20Partnerships%20%28Holland%29.pdf

- *California State University Service-Learning Assessment Plan Rubric*
  www.calstate.edu/cce/initiatives/documents/Goal3_Steps1-8.pdf

- *Campus Compact*
  www.compact.org

- *Center for Civic Reflection*
  civicreflection.org

- *Center for Instructional Excellence at Purdue University, Assessment and Evaluation*
  www.purdue.edu/cie/teaching/assessment-evaluation.html

- *Civic Leadership Initiative Online (CLIO) Minnesota Campus Compact*
  mncampuscompact.org/clio

- *Civic-Minded Graduate, IUPUI*
  csl.iupui.edu/teaching-research/opportunities/civic-learning/graduate.shtml

- *Community Campus Partnerships for Health*
  www.ccph.info

- *Community College National Center for Community Engagement*
  mesacc.edu/other/engagement

- *Community Tool Box, University of Kansas*
  ctb.ku.edu/en

- *Council for the Advancement of Standards in Higher Education*
  www.cas.edu/index.php/about/overview

- *Creating our Identities in Service Learning and Community Engagement*
  www.servicelearning.org/library/resource/8877

- *Deliberative Dialogues through National Issues Forums*
  www.nifi.org

- *Dowser.org, A Quick Guide to Changing the World – Seriously*
  dowser.org/a-quick-guide-to-changing-the-world-seriously

- *Five Good Ideas with Blair Dimock: Mapping Progress, with a Purpose*
  youtube.com/watch?v=iHYTqaBaU4M

- *Freire Institute*
  www.freire.org/paulo-freire

- *Higher Education Research Institute*
  www.heri.ucla.edu

- *Idealist*
  www.idealist.org

- *Imaging America*
  imaginingamerica.org

- *Interfaith Youth Core*
  ifyc.org

- *International Research Conference on Service-Learning and Community Engagement*
  www.researchslce.org

- *LeaderShape*
  www.leadershape.org

- *Minnesota Campus Compact, Assessment and Evaluation Resource*
  mncampuscompact.org/what-we-do/engaged-campuscapacity-building/assessment

- *National Survey of Student Engagement*
  nsse.iub.edu

- *NonprofitGP.com, The Underpinnings of Collective Impact*
  nonprofitgp.com/2012/10/17/the-underpinnings-of-collective-impact

- *OXFAM Change Leader*
  change.oxfamamerica.org

- *The Research University Civic Engagement Network (TRUCEN) Civic Engagement at Research Universities*
  compact.org/initiatives/trucen

- *Social Change Model*
  socialchangemodel.org

- *Strengthening Nonprofits: A Capacity Builder's Resource Library*
  strengtheningnonprofits.org

- *StriveTogether Framework*
  strivetogether.org/strivetogether-approach/strivetogether-framework

- *Teaching for Change*
  teachingforchange.org

- *Volunteering in America Report*
  www.nationalservice.gov/impact-our-nation/research-and-reports/volunteering-america

Conferences

A variety of statewide and regional civic engagement conferences can be found on the National Campus Compact calendar at compact.org. Other ideas for national conferences and convenings:

- *Community Campus Partnership for Health International Conference* www.ccph.info
- *Community College National Center for Community Engagement Conference* www.mesacc.edu/other/engagement
- *Diving Deep: Campus Compact's Institute for Experienced Civic and Community Engagement Practitioners* compact.org/events/ divingdeep
- *Imaging America* imaginingamerica.org/convenings
- *International Association for Research on Service-learning and Community Engagement* www.researchslce.org/conferences
- *NASPA Civic Learning and Democratic Engagement Conference* www.naspa.org/events/2014CLDE
- *National Service-Learning Conference* nslc.nylc.org
- *National Society of Experiential Education* www.nsee.org
- *Virginia Tech Engagement Academy for University Leaders* www.cpe.vt.edu/engagementacademy/eaul

Publication Opportunities in Peer-Reviewed Journals
A complete list can be found on the Campus Compact website:

www.compact.org/category/resources/service-learning-resources/
publishing-outlets-for-service-learning-and-community-based-
research/)

- *Gateways: International Journal of Community Research & Engagement*
- *The International Journal of Research on Service-Learning and Community Engagement*
- *The Journal for Civic Commitment*
- *Journal of Community Engagement and Higher Education*
- *Journal of Higher Education Outreach and Engagement*
- *The Journal of Public Scholarship in Higher Education*
- *Michigan Journal of Community Service Learning*
- *Partnerships: A Journal of Service-Learning and Civic Engagement*
- *PRISM: A Journal of Regional Engagement*
- *Public: A Journal of Imagining America*

Beyond the Typical

Look local. Look for local workshops offered for the nonprofit or business community on topics related to fundraising, resource management, and other management topics. Insurance agencies and other local companies may also offer workshops in risk management that would be useful for overall planning. You can also attend local city council meetings and other input events to learn more about community culture and priorities.

Make connections on campus. Consider other on-campus resources, such as the human resources department and faculty members who may specialize in these areas, including business faculty. They may have resources, be willing to sit down with you, or have a class of students who can help you with a specific project.

Volunteer. Join national or state Campus Compact committees, conference planning committees, award review committees, or as a grant reviewer. Serve a few hours with some of your main community partners (and encourage faculty to do the same).

Connect with colleagues. Participate in professional-development-focused learning communities, online forums, and other opportunities to learn from those in similar positions nationally. You can also be a mentor and find mentors for yourself. Mentoring relationships, whether you are the mentor or mentee, can be great platforms for learning new ideas and ways of thinking.

Seek recognition. Participate in a national ranking or recognition process with your institution, such as Carnegie Classification for community engagement. Participate in the institution's accreditation process in the community engagement area. Apply for and nominate others for state and national awards for volunteerism, service, and community engagement to showcase work and learn about expectations.

Connect online. Social media and other web platforms can allow for broader interaction, new ideas, and new connections.

Conclusion

We hope this publication has given you an opportunity for reflection and, hopefully, conversation. As a field rooted in theories and pedagogies that encourage deep and diverse dialogue and reflection (Giles & Eyler, 1994), we must encourage these practices for ourselves. As we emphasized in the introduction, in addition to the four spheres we have outlined, all community engagement professionals should strive to be reflectors, educators, and communicators. Our goals for this publication are to educate and encourage practitioners to be well-rounded in each of the spheres and overarching practices.

The field of community engagement is young enough to have hope for a bright and challenging future. Only with the last decade has strong dialogue and research developed to grow and change the work of the field (Saltmarsh & Hartley, 2011). For practitioners, we realize reading this cover to cover may raise more questions than answers and inspire feelings of anxiety when thinking about what needs to be accomplished. We hope the resources provided here will allow all professionals to place themselves in the context of the field and their institution and make concrete steps toward further development.

In community engagement, we face a real threat of burnout and other challenges due to the still relatively small number of professionals doing this great work. While the value of community work has increased to $9.7 billion, as of the 2012 Campus Compact Annual Membership Survey, that same survey showed that only 18% of centers and offices had a budget of more than $250,000. We hope this publication communicates the magnitude of the task before us and allows for concrete actions to carry us forward. We also hope it communicates the magnitude of the work to those who make decisions about the allocation of human and fiscal resources. The harsh reality of increasing competition for these resources in higher education is juxtaposed with what we now know from research is the best way to build quality community engagement on campuses. Institutions and professionals need to think creatively about how to meet these challenges head on and ensure that community engagement maintains a high standard of quality. While many of us have been pushing for this work throughout our careers, and much has been accomplished, the fact remains that we have much more work to do. According to just one troubling statistics in the recent *Crucible Moment* report (2012), only one-third of college students believe their education has increased their civic capacities.

Time is often the most valuable resource community engagement professionals can access, and they must guard their own time fiercely. If this publication can serve as a guide for how to spend this valuable resource, we have succeeded. Professionals need to be able to think strategically about how to use the time they have and fight for the right priorities. We ended the book with the sphere of field contributor in the hopes it helps us all to think more about how we can contribute, even in small ways. This is not only needed for the field, but for professionals to continue to grow and be challenged.

Put the book down and step away from your phone and email. We can end where we began: by ***diving deep.*** The time is now, and the urgency is real. Take time to think and steps toward action. Join us in the ocean. Higher education and, indeed, our democracy need you to

...take the plunge.

References

Campus Compact. (2012). *2012 annual membership survey.* Boston, MA.

Giles, D.E.J., & Eyler, J. (1994). The theoretical roots of service-learning in John Dewey: Toward a theory of service-learning. *Michigan Journal of Community Service Learning, 1,* 77-85.

The National Task Force on Civic Learning and Democratic Engagement (2012). *A crucible moment: College learning and democracy's future.* Washington, DC: Association of American Colleges and Universities. Retrieved from http://www.aacu.org/civic_learning/crucible/http://www.aacu.org/civic_learning/crucible/

Saltmarsh, J., & Hartley, M. (2011). *To serve a larger purpose: Engagement for democracy and the transformation of higher education.* Philadelphia, PA: Temple University Press.